January Preschool Curriculum

The Nurtured Path

❄ Winter Learning & Fun

The Nurtured Pathway Curriculum Book
Written and Illustrated by LaShanta Smith

Copyright © 2025, Lashanta Smith
All rights reserved. No part of this publication may be reproduced, stored in a retrieval system or transmitted in any form or by any means, electronic, mechanical, photocopying, recording or otherwise, without prior written permission from the publisher, Engraving Your Views. All rights, reserved, including the right to reproduce this book or portions thereof in any form
ISBN HARDCOVER:979-8-9986389-6-1

Week 1 – New Beginnings

Book of the Week: Squirrel's New Year's Resolution

Monday	Welcome Circle	Read the story and discuss resolutions	Count classmates	Resolution craft	Playdough names	Movement song
Tuesday	Morning Meeting	Story sequencing	Number hunt	New Year hats	Sand table	Freeze dance
Wednesday	Calendar and Weather	Letter S hunt	Counting resolutions	Class collage	Rice bin	Yoga
Thursday	Sharing Time	Story retell	Shape sort	Goal poster	Sensory bins	Parachute play

Friday	Resolution Circle	Story response	Pattern blocks	Friendship bracelets	Water play	Dance party

Week 2 – Snow & Winter Fun

Book of the Week: The Snowy Day

Monday	Greeting Circle	Read The Snowy Day	Counting snowflakes	Snowflake craft	Cotton snow	Snowy dance
Tuesday	Weather Song	Story retell	Number patterns	Winter hat craft	Shaving cream snow	Stretching
Wednesday	Weather Chart	Letter W hunt	Snowman math	Snowman craft	Snow dough	Musical chairs

Thursday	Calendar Time	Story sequencing	Counting mittens	Mitten matching	Ice play	Yoga
Friday	Sharing Time	Story response	Sorting winter clothes	Painting snow	Sensory bottles	Freeze dance

Week 3 – Friendship & Kindness

Book of the Week: Have You Filled a Bucket Today?

Monday	Greeting Circle	Read Bucket Book	Counting hearts	Heart collage	Sand tray	Circle dance
Tuesday	Morning Meeting	Bucket chart	Number match	Friendship mural	Water beads	Movement song

Wednesday	Feelings Chart	Story sequencing	Sharing math	Kindness cards	Rice bin	Parachute fun
Thursday	Calendar Time	Alphabet game	Heart patterns	Handprint art	Playdough hearts	Yoga
Friday	Sharing Circle	Story response	Counting friends	Friendship bracelets	Sensory bottles	Dance party

Week 4 – Hibernation & Animals in Winter

Book of the Week: Bear Snores On

Monday	Greeting Circle	Read Bear Snores On	Counting bears	Bear cave craft	Sand tray	Bear dance

Tuesday	Weather Chart	Story sequencing	Number patterns	Winter animal masks	Snow dough	Stretching
Wednesday	Calendar Time	Letter B hunt	Animal sorting	Hibernation art	Cotton snow	Yoga
Thursday	Sharing Time	Story retell	Animal graphing	Bear collage	Sensory bins	Parachute fun
Friday	Circle Time	Story response	Counting animals	Winter scene mural	Shaving cream play	Dance party

Week 1 – New Beginnings

Book of the Week: Squirrel's New Year's Resolution

Circle Time
Welcome Circle, Morning Meeting, Calendar and Weather, Sharing Time, Resolution Circle

Literacy
Read the story, Story Sequencing, Letter S hunt, Story Retell, Story Response

Math
Counting classmates, Number Hunt, Counting Resolutions, Shape Sort, Pattern Blocks

Art
Resolution Craft, New Year Hats, Class Collage, Goal Poster, Friendship Bracelets

Sensory
Playdough Names, Sand Table, Rice Bin, Sensory Bins, Water Play

Movement
Movement Song, Freeze Dance, Yoga, Parachute Play, Dance Party

Week 2 – Snow & Winter Fun

Book of the Week: The Snowy Day

Circle Time
Greeting Circle, Weather Song, Weather Chart, Calendar Time, Sharing Time

Literacy
Read The Snowy Day, Story Retell, Letter W hunt, Story Sequencing, Story Response

Math
Counting Snowflakes, Number Patterns, Snowman Math, Counting Mittens, Sorting Winter Clothes

Art
Snowflake Craft, Winter Hat Craft, Snowman Craft, Mitten Matching, Painting Snow

Sensory
Cotton Snow, Shaving Cream Snow, Snow Dough, Ice Play, Sensory Bottles

Movement
Snowy Dance, Stretching, Musical Chairs, Yoga, Freeze Dance

Week 3 – Friendship & Kindness

Book of the Week: Have You Filled a Bucket Today?

Circle Time
Greeting Circle, Morning Meeting, Feelings Chart, Calendar Time, Sharing Circle

Literacy
Read Bucket Book, Bucket Chart, Story Sequencing, Alphabet Game, Story Response

Math
Counting Hearts, Number Match, Sharing Math, Heart Patterns, Counting Friends

Art
Heart Collage, Friendship Mural, Kindness Cards, Handprint Art, Friendship Bracelets

Sensory
Sand Tray, Water Beads, Rice Bin, Playdough Hearts, Sensory Bottles

Movement
Circle Dance, Movement Song, Parachute Fun, Yoga, Dance Party

Week 4 – Hibernation & Animals in Winter

Book of the Week: Bear Snores On

Circle Time
Greeting Circle, Weather Chart, Calendar Time, Sharing Time, Circle Time

Literacy
Read Bear Snores On, Story Sequencing, Letter B hunt, Story Retell, Story Response

Math
Counting Bears, Number Patterns, Animal Sorting, Animal Graphing, Counting Animals

Art
Bear Cave Craft, Winter Animal Masks, Hibernation Art, Bear Collage, Winter Scene Mural

Sensory
Sand Tray, Snow Dough, Cotton Snow, Sensory Bins, Shaving Cream Play

Movement
Bear Dance, Stretching, Yoga, Parachute Fun, Dance Party

Week 1 – New Beginnings

Book of the Week: Squirrel's New Year's Resolution

What is something new you want to try this year?

Name: _____

Week 2 – Snow & Winter Fun

Book of the Week: The Snowy Day

What do you like to do in the snow?

Name: _____

Week 3 – Friendship & Kindness

Book of the Week: Have You Filled a Bucket Today?

How can you be kind to a friend?

Name: _____

Week 4 – Hibernation & Animals in Winter

Book of the Week: Bear Snores On

Where would you sleep if you were a bear?

Name: _____

The Nurtured Path – January Preschool Newsletter

Happy New Year and welcome to January at The Nurtured Path! We are excited to begin a fresh year of learning, growing, and having fun together. This month we are exploring new beginnings, snowy adventures, kindness, and hibernating animals. Each week features a special book and hands-on activities that bring learning to life for your child.

This Month's Themes & Books

- Week 1 – New Beginnings: Squirrel's New Year's Resolution
- Week 2 – Snow & Winter Fun: The Snowy Day
- Week 3 – Friendship & Kindness: Have You Filled a Bucket Today?
- Week 4 – Hibernation & Animals in Winter: Bear Snores On

Classroom Highlights

This month our preschoolers will make New Year's resolution crafts, build snowmen from paper and cotton, create bucket-filling kindness cards, and design bear caves for our winter animals unit. We will also enjoy winter sensory play such as snow dough, shaving cream snow, and water beads. Through music, art, movement, and storytelling, children will practice important social-emotional skills while having fun.

Important Reminders

- Please send your child with warm outdoor clothing every day – coats, hats, mittens, and boots. • Label all clothing to prevent mix-ups. • School will be closed on Martin Luther King Jr. Day. • Healthy snacks are encouraged – please avoid sugary treats. • Check your child's cubby each week for artwork and important notes.

Looking Ahead to February

In February we will celebrate friendship and Valentine's Day, learn about colors and shapes, and continue exploring creativity through crafts, songs, and group activities. It will be a month filled with love and learning!

Thank you for being part of The Nurtured Path family. Together we are making this a joyful and inclusive place for every chi

February Preschool Curriculum

The Nurtured Path

♥ Friendship, Love & Learning ♥

Week 1 – Friendship & Love

Book of the Week: The Day It Rained Hearts

Monday	Welcome Circle	Read story	Counting hearts	Heart craft	Sand tray	Friendship song
Tuesday	Morning Meeting	Story sequencing	Number match	Collage	Water beads	Freeze dance
Wednesday	Calendar and Weather	Letter H hunt	Heart patterns	Card making	Playdough hearts	Yoga
Thursday	Sharing Time	Story retell	Counting friends	Handprint art	Rice bin	Parachute play

| Friday | Friendship Circle | Story response | Sorting hearts | Friendship bracelets | Sensory bottles | Dance party |

Week 2 – Valentine's Fun

Book of the Week: Pete the Cat: Valentine's Day Is Cool

Monday	Greeting Circle	Read Pete the Cat	Counting valentines	Valentine cards	Cotton snow	Movement song
Tuesday	Morning Meeting	Story retell	Number patterns	Heart mural	Shaving cream play	Stretching
Wednesday	Weather Chart	Letter V hunt	Counting valentines	Painting hearts	Sensory bin	Yoga

Thursday	Calendar Time	Story sequencing	Sorting cards	Craft bags	Water play	Parachute fun
Friday	Sharing Time	Story response	Graphing favorites	Cookie decorating	Sensory bottles	Dance party

Week 3 – Colors & Shapes

Book of the Week: Mouse Shapes

Monday	Welcome Circle	Read Mouse Shapes	Sorting shapes	Shape collage	Sand tray	Movement song
Tuesday	Morning Meeting	Story retell	Counting shapes	Painting shapes	Playdough shapes	Yoga

Wednesday	Calendar and Weather	Letter S hunt	Shape matching	Shape mural	Rice bin	Stretching
Thursday	Sharing Time	Story sequencing	Graphing colors	Color painting	Water beads	Freeze dance
Friday	Circle Time	Story response	Pattern making	Color collage	Sensory bottles	Dance party

Week 4 – Community Helpers

Book of the Week: Whose Hat Is This?

Monday	Greeting Circle	Read story	Counting hats	Hat craft	Sand tray	Movement song

Day							
Tuesday	Morning Meeting	Story sequencing	Number match	Badge craft	Shaving cream play	Yoga	
Wednesday	Calendar Time	Letter H hunt	Sorting jobs	Collage	Water play	Stretching	
Thursday	Sharing Time	Story retell	Graphing jobs	Community mural	Rice bin	Parachute fun	
Friday	Community Circle	Story response	Counting tools	Dress-up play	Sensory bottles	Dance party	

Week 1 – Friendship & Love

Book of the Week: The Day It Rained Hearts

Circle Time
Welcome Circle, Morning Meeting, Calendar and Weather, Sharing Time, Friendship Circle

Literacy
Read story, Story Sequencing, Letter H hunt, Story Retell, Story Response

Math
Counting hearts, Number Match, Heart Patterns, Counting Friends, Sorting Hearts

Art
Heart Craft, Collage, Card Making, Handprint Art, Friendship Bracelets

Sensory
Sand Tray, Water Beads, Playdough Hearts, Rice Bin, Sensory Bottles

Movement
Friendship Song, Freeze Dance, Yoga, Parachute Play, Dance Party

Week 2 – Valentine's Fun

Book of the Week: Pete the Cat: Valentine's Day Is Cool

Circle Time
Greeting Circle, Morning Meeting, Weather Chart, Calendar Time, Sharing Time

Literacy
Read Pete the Cat, Story Retell, Letter V Hunt, Story Sequencing, Story Response

Math
Counting Valentines, Number Patterns, Counting Valentines, Sorting Cards, Graphing Favorites

Art
Valentine Cards, Heart Mural, Painting Hearts, Craft Bags, Cookie Decorating

Sensory
Cotton Snow, Shaving Cream Play, Sensory Bin, Water Play, Sensory Bottles

Movement
Movement Song, Stretching, Yoga, Parachute Fun, Dance Party

Week 3 – Colors & Shapes

Book of the Week: Mouse Shapes

Circle Time
Welcome Circle, Morning Meeting, Calendar and Weather, Sharing Time, Circle Time

Literacy
Read Mouse Shapes, Story Retell, Letter S Hunt, Story Sequencing, Story Response

Math
Sorting Shapes, Counting Shapes, Shape Matching, Graphing Colors, Pattern Making

Art
Shape Collage, Painting Shapes, Shape Mural, Color Painting, Color Collage

Sensory
Sand Tray, Playdough Shapes, Rice Bin, Water Beads, Sensory Bottles

Movement
Movement Song, Yoga, Stretching, Freeze Dance, Dance Party

Week 4 – Community Helpers

Book of the Week: Whose Hat Is This?

Circle Time
Greeting Circle, Morning Meeting, Calendar Time, Sharing Time, Community Circle

Literacy
Read story, Story Sequencing, Letter H Hunt, Story Retell, Story Response

Math
Counting Hats, Number Match, Sorting Jobs, Graphing Jobs, Counting Tools

Art
Hat Craft, Badge Craft, Collage, Community Mural, Dress-up Play

Sensory
Sand Tray, Shaving Cream Play, Water Play, Rice Bin, Sensory Bottles

Movement
Movement Song, Yoga, Stretching, Parachute Fun, Dance Party

Week 1 – Friendship & Love: Monday

Circle Time

Begin with a welcome song. Talk about friends and love. Introduce the book The Day It Rained Hearts.

Literacy

Read the book aloud. Pause to show the pictures and ask children what they see raining from the sky.

Math

Count paper hearts together. Practice numbers 1–10 by placing hearts on the board.

Art

Make heart crafts using colored paper, glue, and glitter.

Sensory

Fill a bin with red rice and small plastic hearts for children to scoop and pour.

Movement

Sing and dance to a friendship song while clapping and moving in a circle.

Week 1 – Friendship & Love: Tuesday

Circle Time
Start with morning greetings. Talk about sharing and giving valentines.

Literacy
Retell The Day It Rained Hearts with picture cards. Let children place cards in order.

Math
Match number cards with the correct number of hearts.

Art
Create a class collage of hearts using paint and markers.

Sensory
Add water beads to a bin for a soft sensory experience.

Movement
Play Freeze Dance with cheerful music. Children freeze like statues when music stops.

Week 1 – Friendship & Love: Wednesday

Circle Time
Check the calendar and weather. Sing a song about the weather and seasons.

Literacy
Letter Hunt – look for the letter H (for Heart) around the classroom.

Math
Make heart patterns (red, pink, red, pink). Extend with AB or ABC patterns.

Art
Decorate valentines with stickers and crayons.

Sensory
Provide playdough to roll and cut into heart shapes.

Movement
Practice yoga poses such as 'reach for the stars' and 'heart opener' stretch.

Week 1 – Friendship & Love: Thursday

Circle Time
Sharing Time – children share how they show kindness to others.

Literacy
Retell the story with children acting out the parts.

Math
Count classmates and talk about being kind to each one.

Art
Make handprint art to create a friendship tree on poster board.

Sensory
Rice bin with hidden heart cutouts for children to find.

Movement
Parachute play – toss paper hearts into the air and catch them with the parachute.

Week 1 – Friendship & Love: Friday

Circle Time
Friendship Circle – talk about favorite things to do with friends.

Literacy
Draw a picture response to the story. Children share their drawings with the group.

Math
Sort paper hearts by color and size.

Art
Make friendship bracelets with beads and yarn.

Sensory
Fill bottles with glitter, water, and sequins to make calming sensory bottles.

Movement
End the week with a fun dance party to celebrate friendship and love.

Week 2 – Valentine's Fun: Monday

Circle Time

Start with greetings. Talk about Valentine's Day and why we give cards.

Literacy

Read Pete the Cat: Valentine's Day Is Cool. Discuss Pete's friends and why he likes Valentine's.

Math

Count valentines together. Practice writing numbers 1–10 on heart shapes.

Art

Make Valentine cards with stickers, crayons, and doilies.

Sensory

Play with cotton ball 'snow' and plastic hearts in a bin.

Movement

Sing a Valentine's song and move like dancing hearts.

Week 2 – Valentine's Fun: Tuesday

Circle Time
Morning meeting. Share favorite colors and talk about heart colors.

Literacy
Retell Pete the Cat's story with picture cards. Children place events in order.

Math
Practice number patterns using red and pink hearts.

Art
Make a heart mural where children add their decorated hearts to a large paper.

Sensory
Use shaving cream on trays to draw hearts and letters.

Movement
Stretch tall like a tower of valentines, then curl small like a heart.

Week 2 – Valentine's Fun: Wednesday

Circle Time
Weather chart. Talk about winter weather and holidays like Valentine's.

Literacy
Letter Hunt – find the letter V for Valentine around the room.

Math
Count and sort valentines by size and color.

Art
Paint hearts with brushes or sponges.

Sensory
Fill a bin with rice and hidden Valentine cards to find.

Movement
Practice yoga poses such as 'heart opener' and 'tree pose'.

Week 2 – Valentine's Fun: Thursday

Circle Time
Calendar time. Discuss how many days until Valentine's Day.

Literacy
Story sequencing – retell Pete's Valentine's Day adventures.

Math
Sort and graph favorite Valentine cards.

Art
Decorate Valentine bags to collect cards.

Sensory
Water play with floating heart shapes and cups.

Movement
Parachute play with paper valentines tossed in the air.

Week 2 – Valentine's Fun: Friday

Circle Time
Sharing time – talk about what makes friends special.

Literacy
Story response – draw a picture of your favorite part of Pete's Valentine story.

Math
Graph the class's favorite Valentine treat or color.

Art
Decorate cookies with frosting and sprinkles.

Sensory
Make Valentine sensory bottles with glitter and confetti.

Movement
End the week with a Valentine dance party with music.

Week 3 – Colors & Shapes: Monday

Circle Time
Welcome song. Talk about shapes children already know (circle, square, triangle).

Literacy
Read Mouse Shapes. Pause to discuss what shapes the mice use in the story.

Math
Sort blocks or cutouts by shape. Count how many circles, squares, and triangles.

Art
Make a shape collage with construction paper.

Sensory
Sand tray with shape stamps or cookie cutters.

Movement
Play a movement game: when the teacher calls 'circle,' children make a circle with their arms.

Week 3 – Colors & Shapes: Tuesday

Circle Time
Morning meeting. Show shape flashcards and have children name them.

Literacy
Retell Mouse Shapes with puppets or props. Children help act out the story.

Math
Count and sort shapes by color. Practice grouping items together.

Art
Paint with shape sponges (circle, square, triangle).

Sensory
Playdough shapes – roll and cut with shape cutters.

Movement
Yoga: make body poses like shapes (triangle pose, star pose).

Week 3 – Colors & Shapes: Wednesday

Circle Time
Calendar and weather. Talk about shapes we see in the classroom.

Literacy
Letter Hunt – look for the letter S for Shapes.

Math
Match shapes to outlines. Talk about sides and corners.

Art
Create a class mural of a town made from different shapes.

Sensory
Rice bin with hidden foam shapes to find and name.

Movement
Stretch arms and legs wide like a star, then curl small like a ball (circle).

Week 3 – Colors & Shapes: Thursday

Circle Time
Sharing time. Children share their favorite shape and why.

Literacy
Story sequencing – put Mouse Shapes events in order with cards.

Math
Graph favorite shapes in class. Count how many circles, squares, triangles.

Art
Paint with many colors to decorate shape outlines.

Sensory
Water beads with floating foam shapes.

Movement
Freeze dance – freeze into a shape when music stops.

Week 3 – Colors & Shapes: Friday

Circle Time
Circle song. Review shapes learned this week.

Literacy
Story response – draw a picture of something made with shapes.

Math
Make repeating patterns with shapes (circle, square, circle, square).

Art
Color collage – glue different colors of paper onto shapes.

Sensory
Sensory bottles filled with beads and foam shapes.

Movement
Dance party – children dance and make shapes with their arms and bodies.

Week 4 – Community Helpers: Monday

Circle Time
Welcome circle. Talk about community helpers and why they are important.

Literacy
Read Whose Hat Is This?. Pause to let children guess which helper wears each hat.

Math
Count toy hats or pictures of hats together. Practice numbers 1–10.

Art
Make paper hats (firefighter, chef, builder) and decorate with crayons.

Sensory
Fill a bin with hats and job-related items for children to explore.

Movement
March like firefighters, walk like police officers, pretend to fly like pilots.

Week 4 – Community Helpers: Tuesday

Circle Time
Morning meeting. Share about family members who have jobs.

Literacy
Story sequencing – retell Whose Hat Is This? with picture cards.

Math
Match job tools to the right community helper (e.g., stethoscope – doctor).

Art
Create badges for police officers or name tags for helpers.

Sensory
Use shaving cream as 'firefighting foam' for messy play.

Movement
Pretend play – act out jobs such as cooking, building, or helping people.

Week 4 – Community Helpers: Wednesday

Circle Time
Calendar and weather. Discuss which helpers work in different weather.

Literacy
Letter Hunt – find the letter H for Hat and Helper.

Math
Sort pictures of community helpers by category (medical, safety, food).

Art
Make a collage of community helper hats using magazine cutouts.

Sensory
Water play with toy boats and rescue figures.

Movement
Practice yoga poses – strong like a builder, balanced like a doctor, calm like a teacher.

Week 4 – Community Helpers: Thursday

Circle Time
Sharing Time – children share what they want to be when they grow up.

Literacy
Story retell – act out Whose Hat Is This? with hats and props.

Math
Graph favorite community helpers in the class.

Art
Create a community mural with drawings of helpers at work.

Sensory
Rice bin with hidden job tools for children to find.

Movement
Parachute play – pretend the parachute is a big firefighter's hose spraying water.

Week 4 – Community Helpers: Friday

Circle Time
Community Circle – review what we learned about helpers.

Literacy
Story response – children draw their favorite community helper.

Math
Count tools or hats brought to class. Practice simple addition (2 hats + 3 hats = 5).

Art
Dress-up play with hats, vests, and pretend tools.

Sensory
Sensory bottles with items representing helpers (toy hats, mini tools).

Movement
Dance party – move like different helpers (march like police, fly like pilot).

Week 1 – Friendship & Love

Book of the Week: The Day It Rained Hearts

What would you do if hearts rained from the sky?

Name: _____

Week 2 – Valentine's Fun

Book of the Week: Pete the Cat: Valentine's

Day Is Cool Who would you give a valentine

to?

Name: _____

Week 3 – Colors & Shapes

Book of the Week: Mouse Shapes

What can you make using shapes?

Name: _____

Week 4 – Community Helpers

Book of the Week: Whose Hat Is This?

What do you want to be when you grow up?

Name: _____

The Nurtured Path – February Preschool Newsletter

February is full of love, kindness, and creativity! This month our preschoolers are celebrating friendship, enjoying Valentine's fun, exploring colors and shapes, and learning about community helpers. Through stories, crafts, and play, children will discover how to be kind friends, express their creativity, and understand the roles of helpers in our community.

This Month's Themes & Books

- Week 1 – Friendship & Love: The Day It Rained Hearts
- Week 2 – Valentine's Fun: Pete the Cat: Valentine's Day Is Cool
- Week 3 – Colors & Shapes: Mouse Shapes
- Week 4 – Community Helpers: Whose Hat Is This?

Classroom Highlights

• Creating heart crafts, collages, and valentines to share • Retelling stories with puppets and picture cards • Building patterns and murals with shapes • Exploring jobs and making a community helper mural • Enjoying sensory play with rice bins, playdough, and water beads

Important Reminders

• Valentine's Day party will be held on February 14 – please bring valentines to share. • Remember to dress warmly for outdoor play in winter weather. • Please label all coats, hats, and mittens. • Look out for notes about our community helpers week activities.

Looking Ahead to March

In March we will celebrate springtime, explore weather changes, and learn about growth in plants and animals. Get ready for a month filled with curiosity and discovery!

Thank you for being part of The Nurtured Path family. We look forward to another month of joy and learning together!

March Preschool Curriculum

The Nurtured Path

■ Spring into Learning ■

Week 1 – Spring & Weather

Book of the Week: When Spring Comes

Monday	Welcome Circle	Read story	Count flowers	Flower craft	Sand tray	Spring song
Tuesday	Morning Meeting	Story sequencing	Number match	Rainbow art	Water beads	Freeze dance
Wednesday	Calendar & Weather	Letter S hunt	Counting raindrops	Rain craft	Playdough flowers	Yoga
Thursday	Sharing Time	Story retell	Weather graphing	Spring collage	Rice bin	Parachute play

| Friday | Spring Circle | Story response | Sorting weather cards | Butterfly craft | Sensory bottles | Dance party |

Week 2 – Rainbows & Colors

Book of the Week: A Rainbow of My Own

Monday	Greeting Circle	Read Rainbow book	Color counting	Rainbow painting	Cotton balls	Movement song
Tuesday	Morning Meeting	Story retell	Color patterns	Rainbow collage	Shaving cream rainbows	Stretching
Wednesday	Weather Chart	Letter R hunt	Sorting colors	Rainbow mural	Sensory bin	Yoga

Day						
Thursday	Calendar Time	Story sequencing	Counting colors	Rainbow wands	Water play	Parachute fun
Friday	Sharing Time	Story response	Graphing favorite colors	Color mixing	Sensory bottles	Dance party

Week 3 – St. Patrick's & Luck

Book of the Week: How to Catch a Leprechaun

Day						
Monday	Welcome Circle	Read Leprechaun story	Counting gold coins	Leprechaun trap craft	Sand tray	Irish jig dance
Tuesday	Morning Meeting	Story sequencing	Number hunt	Rainbow hats	Water beads	Freeze dance

Wednesday	Calendar & Weather	Letter L hunt	Sorting shamrocks	Pot of gold art	Playdough shamrocks	Yoga
Thursday	Sharing Time	Story retell	Graphing lucky charms	Gold coin mural	Rice bin	Parachute play
Friday	Lucky Circle	Story response	Patterning coins	Leprechaun hats	Sensory bottles	Dance party

Week 4 – Growing Plants

Book of the Week: The Tiny Seed

Monday	Greeting Circle	Read Tiny Seed	Counting seeds	Seed collage	Soil sensory bin	Movement song

Tuesday	Morning Meeting	Story sequencing	Number graphing	Planting craft	Water play	Stretching
Wednesday	Calendar & Weather	Letter P hunt	Measuring plants	Flower mural	Rice bin	Yoga
Thursday	Sharing Time	Story retell	Sorting seeds	Garden craft	Sand tray	Parachute fun
Friday	Plant Circle	Story response	Counting flowers	Garden mural	Sensory bottles	Dance party

Week 1 – Spring & Weather

Book of the Week: When Spring Comes

Circle Time
Welcome Circle, Morning Meeting, Calendar & Weather, Sharing Time, Spring Circle

Literacy
Read story, Story Sequencing, Letter S Hunt, Story Retell, Story Response

Math
Count Flowers, Number Match, Counting Raindrops, Weather Graphing, Sorting Weather Cards

Art
Flower Craft, Rainbow Art, Rain Craft, Spring Collage, Butterfly Craft

Sensory
Sand Tray, Water Beads, Playdough Flowers, Rice Bin, Sensory Bottles

Movement
Spring Song, Freeze Dance, Yoga, Parachute Play, Dance Party

Week 2 – Rainbows & Colors

Book of the Week: A Rainbow of My Own

Circle Time
Greeting Circle, Morning Meeting, Weather Chart, Calendar Time, Sharing Time

Literacy
Read Rainbow Book, Story Retell, Letter R Hunt, Story Sequencing, Story Response

Math
Color Counting, Color Patterns, Sorting Colors, Counting Colors, Graphing Favorite Colors

Art
Rainbow Painting, Rainbow Collage, Rainbow Mural, Rainbow Wands, Color Mixing

Sensory
Cotton Balls, Shaving Cream Rainbows, Sensory Bin, Water Play, Sensory Bottles

Movement
Movement Song, Stretching, Yoga, Parachute Fun, Dance Party

Week 3 – St. Patrick's & Luck

Book of the Week: How to Catch a Leprechaun

Circle Time
Welcome Circle, Morning Meeting, Calendar & Weather, Sharing Time, Lucky Circle

Literacy
Read Leprechaun Story, Story Sequencing, Letter L Hunt, Story Retell, Story Response

Math
Counting Coins, Number Hunt, Sorting Shamrocks, Graphing Lucky Charms, Patterning Coins

Art
Leprechaun Trap Craft, Rainbow Hats, Pot of Gold Art, Gold Coin Mural, Leprechaun Hats

Sensory
Sand Tray, Water Beads, Playdough Shamrocks, Rice Bin, Sensory Bottles

Movement
Irish Jig Dance, Freeze Dance, Yoga, Parachute Play, Dance Party

Week 4 – Growing Plants

Book of the Week: The Tiny Seed

Circle Time
Greeting Circle, Morning Meeting, Calendar & Weather, Sharing Time, Plant Circle

Literacy
Read Tiny Seed, Story Sequencing, Letter P Hunt, Story Retell, Story Response

Math
Counting Seeds, Number Graphing, Measuring Plants, Sorting Seeds, Counting Flowers

Art
Seed Collage, Planting Craft, Flower Mural, Garden Craft, Garden Mural

Sensory
Soil Bin, Water Play, Rice Bin, Sand Tray, Sensory Bottles

Movement
Movement Song, Stretching, Yoga, Parachute Fun, Dance Party

Week 1 – Spring & Weather: Monday

Circle Time
Welcome song. Talk about signs of spring. Introduce the book When Spring Comes.

Literacy
Read the story aloud. Ask children what changes they notice in spring.

Math
Count flower cutouts together. Practice numbers 1–10.

Art
Make paper flowers using tissue paper and glue.

Sensory
Sand tray with toy flowers to dig and plant.

Movement
Sing and dance to a spring song while pretending to be growing plants.

Week 1 – Spring & Weather: Tuesday

Circle Time
Morning greetings. Talk about rain and how it helps plants grow.

Literacy
Story sequencing – retell When Spring Comes with picture cards.

Math
Match numbers with raindrop cutouts.

Art
Paint a rainbow with watercolors.

Sensory
Water beads for rainy day sensory play.

Movement
Play Freeze Dance pretending to be raindrops falling from the sky.

Week 1 – Spring & Weather: Wednesday

Circle Time
Calendar and weather check. Talk about sunny, rainy, and cloudy days.

Literacy
Letter Hunt – find the letter S for Spring in the classroom.

Math
Count paper raindrops and compare amounts (more/less).

Art
Create rain cloud crafts with cotton balls and blue paper.

Sensory
Playdough flowers – roll and shape petals and stems.

Movement
Practice yoga poses – tree pose, flower pose.

Week 1 – Spring & Weather: Thursday

Circle Time
Sharing Time – children share their favorite thing about spring.

Literacy
Story retell – children act out parts of When Spring Comes.

Math
Graph weather types (sunny, rainy, cloudy) with class votes.

Art
Make a spring collage with magazines or colored paper.

Sensory
Rice bin with hidden flower and butterfly cutouts.

Movement
Parachute play – toss tissue paper flowers into the air.

Week 1 – Spring & Weather: Friday

Circle Time
Spring Circle – review what we learned about spring.

Literacy
Story response – children draw their favorite spring activity.

Math
Sort weather cards (sunny, rainy, cloudy, snowy).

Art
Make butterfly crafts with coffee filters and markers.

Sensory
Sensory bottles with glitter, water, and flower sequins.

Movement
End the week with a spring dance party.

Week 2 – Rainbows & Colors: Monday

Circle Time
Greeting circle. Talk about rainbows and what colors we see in them.

Literacy
Read A Rainbow of My Own. Ask children what they would do with their own rainbow.

Math
Count rainbow color strips together. Practice sequencing colors in order.

Art
Paint a rainbow using watercolor paints.

Sensory
Cotton balls in a bin for 'clouds' with rainbow ribbons.

Movement
Sing a rainbow song while stretching arms into arch shapes.

Week 2 – Rainbows & Colors: Tuesday

Circle Time
Morning meeting. Discuss favorite colors.

Literacy
Retell the rainbow story with felt board pieces.

Math
Make repeating color patterns (red-blue-red-blue).

Art
Create a rainbow collage with colored paper scraps.

Sensory
Shaving cream play – swirl in food coloring to make rainbow designs.

Movement
Stretch and move like different rainbow colors (red = strong, blue = calm).

Week 2 – Rainbows & Colors: Wednesday

Circle Time
Calendar and weather check. Talk about when rainbows appear.

Literacy
Letter Hunt – find the letter R for Rainbow around the classroom.

Math
Sort classroom objects by color groups.

Art
Make a class rainbow mural together.

Sensory
Sensory bin with colorful beads and scoops.

Movement
Practice yoga rainbow pose – arch back gently like a rainbow.

Week 2 – Rainbows & Colors: Thursday

Circle Time
Sharing time – children share their favorite rainbow color.

Literacy
Story sequencing – children put rainbow story cards in order.

Math
Count how many of each color are in a pile of blocks or counters.

Art
Make rainbow wands with ribbons and sticks.

Sensory
Water play – drop food coloring in cups of water to mix rainbow colors.

Movement
Parachute play – lift and wave a rainbow parachute together.

Week 2 – Rainbows & Colors: Friday

Circle Time
Review rainbows and colors. Sing a rainbow song together.

Literacy
Story response – draw a picture of what they would do with their own rainbow.

Math
Graph class favorite colors on a chart.

Art
Color mixing activity with paints to create new shades.

Sensory
Sensory bottles with rainbow glitter and sequins.

Movement
Dance party – children dance with rainbow scarves or ribbons.

Week 3 – St. Patrick's & Luck: Monday

Circle Time
Welcome circle. Introduce St. Patrick's Day and leprechauns.

Literacy
Read How to Catch a Leprechaun. Ask children how they would catch one.

Math
Count gold coins together. Practice simple addition with coins.

Art
Make leprechaun traps with cardboard and craft supplies.

Sensory
Sand tray with hidden gold coins for children to dig up.

Movement
Learn an Irish jig dance to celebrate St. Patrick's Day.

Week 3 – St. Patrick's & Luck: Tuesday

Circle Time
Morning greetings. Talk about lucky symbols (clovers, rainbows).

Literacy
Story sequencing – retell How to Catch a Leprechaun with picture cards.

Math
Number hunt – children search for shamrock numbers around the room.

Art
Make rainbow hats using construction paper strips.

Sensory
Water beads in green and gold for sensory play.

Movement
Play Freeze Dance pretending to be sneaky leprechauns.

Week 3 – St. Patrick's & Luck: Wednesday

Circle Time
Calendar and weather. Talk about spring weather and rainbows.

Literacy
Letter Hunt – find the letter L for Leprechaun in the classroom.

Math
Sort shamrocks by size and color. Count how many of each.

Art
Create pots of gold with paper and glitter.

Sensory
Playdough shamrocks – roll and cut with shamrock cutters.

Movement
Yoga poses – rainbow arch, tree pose (shamrock).

Week 3 – St. Patrick's & Luck: Thursday

Circle Time
Sharing time – children share how they would trick a leprechaun.

Literacy
Story retell – children act out parts of the leprechaun story.

Math
Graph lucky charms (favorite symbols) with class votes.

Art
Make a class mural of rainbows and gold.

Sensory
Rice bin with hidden shamrocks and coins.

Movement
Parachute play – toss gold coins and shamrocks in the air.

Week 3 – St. Patrick's & Luck: Friday

Circle Time
Lucky Circle – talk about what makes us feel lucky.

Literacy
Story response – children draw their favorite part of How to Catch a Leprechaun.

Math
Practice patterning with gold coins (gold-green-gold-green).

Art
Make leprechaun hats with green paper and buckles.

Sensory
Sensory bottles with gold glitter and shamrock confetti.

Movement
Dance party – children dance like leprechauns to Irish music.

Week 4 – Growing Plants: Monday

Circle Time
Greeting circle. Talk about how seeds grow into plants.

Literacy
Read The Tiny Seed. Ask children what happens to the seed in the story.

Math
Count real seeds together. Practice sorting by size.

Art
Make seed collages by gluing seeds to paper.

Sensory
Soil bin with scoops and toy seeds to plant.

Movement
Sing and act out 'I'm a Little Seed' while curling small and stretching tall.

Week 4 – Growing Plants: Tuesday

Circle Time
Morning meeting. Discuss what plants need to grow (sun, water, soil).

Literacy
Story sequencing – retell The Tiny Seed with picture cards.

Math
Graph how many children like flowers, trees, or vegetables best.

Art
Create planting crafts with paper cups and markers.

Sensory
Water play – pretend to water toy plants with cups and watering cans.

Movement
Stretch like a growing plant – start small and grow tall.

Week 4 – Growing Plants: Wednesday

Circle Time
Calendar and weather. Talk about how weather helps plants grow.

Literacy
Letter Hunt – find the letter P for Plant in the classroom.

Math
Measure pretend plants with rulers or blocks.

Art
Paint a flower mural together as a class.

Sensory
Rice bin with hidden seeds and flower figures.

Movement
Yoga poses – tree pose, flower pose.

Week 4 – Growing Plants: Thursday

Circle Time
Sharing Time – children share what plants they have seen or grown.

Literacy
Story retell – act out the journey of The Tiny Seed.

Math
Sort seeds by type (beans, sunflower, corn).

Art
Make garden crafts with construction paper and stickers.

Sensory
Sand tray – bury and dig for seed cutouts.

Movement
Parachute play – pretend the parachute is the sun shining on plants.

Week 4 – Growing Plants: Friday

Circle Time
Plant Circle – review what we learned about seeds and plants.

Literacy
Story response – children draw their favorite part of The Tiny Seed.

Math
Count flowers and match numbers to quantities.

Art
Make a garden mural with paper flowers and leaves.

Sensory
Sensory bottles with seeds, water, and glitter.

Movement
Dance party – pretend to be growing plants swaying in the wind.

Week 1 – Spring & Weather

Book of the Week: When Spring Comes

What do you like about spring?

Name: _____

Week 2 – Rainbows & Colors

Book of the Week: A Rainbow of My Own

What would you do with your own rainbow?

Name: _____

Week 3 – St. Patrick's & Luck

Book of the Week: How to Catch a Leprechaun

How would you catch a leprechaun?

Name: _____

Week 4 – Growing Plants

Book of the Week: The Tiny Seed

What do plants need to grow?

Name: _____

The Nurtured Path – March Preschool Newsletter

March brings the excitement of spring! This month our preschoolers are exploring weather changes, rainbows, lucky leprechauns, and how seeds grow into plants. Through engaging stories, creative art projects, and hands-on activities, children will learn about growth, colors, and the world around them.

This Month's Themes & Books

- Week 1 – Spring & Weather: When Spring Comes
- Week 2 – Rainbows & Colors: A Rainbow of My Own
- Week 3 – St. Patrick's & Luck: How to Catch a Leprechaun
- Week 4 – Growing Plants: The Tiny Seed

Classroom Highlights

- Painting rainbows and making rainbow wands • Building leprechaun traps and gold coin art • Planting seeds and learning what plants need to grow • Exploring sensory bins with colorful beads, water play, and soil • Singing and dancing to celebrate springtime

Important Reminders

- Please bring light jackets as the weather changes. • St. Patrick's Day celebration will be held on March 17. • We will be planting seeds – donations of soil, seeds, or small pots are welcome. • Remember to label coats, hats, and water bottles.

Looking Ahead to April

In April we will learn about baby animals, celebrate Easter fun, and take care of our Earth on Earth Day. It will be a month of curiosity and care for nature!

Thank you for being part of The Nurtured Path family. We look forward to another month of joy and learning together!

April Preschool Curriculum The Nurtured Path

■ Growing Together in April ■

Week 1 – Baby Animals

Book of the Week: Are You My Mother?

Monday	Welcome Circle	Read story	Counting animals	Animal craft	Sand tray	Animal song
Tuesday	Morning Meeting	Story sequencing	Number match	Nest craft	Water beads	Freeze dance
Wednesday	Calendar & Weather	Letter A hunt	Counting eggs	Farm collage	Playdough animals	Yoga
Thursday	Sharing Time	Story retell	Graph animals	Baby animal art	Rice bin	Parachute play

Friday	Animal Circle	Story response	Sorting animals	Animal masks	Sensory bottles	Dance party

Week 2 – Easter & Springtime

Book of the Week: The Easter Egg

Monday	Greeting Circle	Read story	Counting eggs	Egg decorating	Cotton balls	Movement song
Tuesday	Morning Meeting	Story retell	Egg patterns	Easter basket craft	Shaving cream eggs	Stretching
Wednesday	Weather Chart	Letter E hunt	Sorting eggs	Egg mural	Sensory bin	Yoga

| Thursday | Calendar Time | Story sequencing | Counting bunnies | Bunny craft | Water play | Parachute fun |
| Friday | Sharing Time | Story response | Graphing egg colors | Spring art | Sensory bottles | Dance party |

Week 3 – Earth Day & Nature

Book of the Week: The Earth Book

Monday	Welcome Circle	Read Earth Book	Counting trees	Earth collage	Sand tray	Nature walk
Tuesday	Morning Meeting	Story sequencing	Number hunt	Recycle craft	Water beads	Freeze dance

Wednesday	Calendar & Weather	Letter E hunt	Sorting trash/recycle	Earth mural	Playdough Earth	Yoga
Thursday	Sharing Time	Story retell	Graph recycling	Nature craft	Rice bin	Parachute play
Friday	Earth Circle	Story response	Counting plants	Earth art	Sensory bottles	Dance party

Week 4 – Gardens & Growth

Book of the Week: Planting a Rainbow

Monday	Greeting Circle	Read story	Counting flowers	Flower painting	Soil bin	Movement song

Tuesday	Morning Meeting	Story sequencing	Number graphing	Garden craft	Water play	Stretching
Wednesday	Calendar & Weather	Letter G hunt	Measuring plants	Garden mural	Rice bin	Yoga
Thursday	Sharing Time	Story retell	Sorting seeds	Flower craft	Sand tray	Parachute fun
Friday	Garden Circle	Story response	Graphing flowers	Rainbow mural	Sensory bottles	Dance party

Week 1 – Baby Animals

Book of the Week: Are You My Mother?

Circle Time
Welcome Circle, Morning Meeting, Calendar & Weather, Sharing Time, Animal Circle

Literacy
Read story, Story Sequencing, Letter A Hunt, Story Retell, Story Response

Math
Counting animals, Number Match, Counting eggs, Graph animals, Sorting animals

Art
Animal Craft, Nest Craft, Farm Collage, Baby Animal Art, Animal Masks

Sensory
Sand Tray, Water Beads, Playdough Animals, Rice Bin, Sensory Bottles

Movement
Animal Song, Freeze Dance, Yoga, Parachute Play, Dance Party

Week 2 – Easter & Springtime

Book of the Week: The Easter Egg

Circle Time
Greeting Circle, Morning Meeting, Weather Chart, Calendar Time, Sharing Time

Literacy
Read story, Story Retell, Letter E Hunt, Story Sequencing, Story Response

Math
Counting eggs, Egg Patterns, Sorting eggs, Counting bunnies, Graphing egg colors

Art
Egg Decorating, Basket Craft, Egg Mural, Bunny Craft, Spring Art

Sensory
Cotton Balls, Shaving Cream Eggs, Sensory Bin, Water Play, Sensory Bottles

Movement
Movement Song, Stretching, Yoga, Parachute Fun, Dance Party

Week 3 – Earth Day & Nature

Book of the Week: The Earth Book

Circle Time
Welcome Circle, Morning Meeting, Calendar & Weather, Sharing Time, Earth Circle

Literacy
Read Earth Book, Story Sequencing, Letter E Hunt, Story Retell, Story Response

Math
Counting Trees, Number Hunt, Sorting Trash/Recycle, Graph Recycling, Counting Plants

Art
Earth Collage, Recycle Craft, Earth Mural, Nature Craft, Earth Art

Sensory
Sand Tray, Water Beads, Playdough Earth, Rice Bin, Sensory Bottles

Movement
Nature Walk, Freeze Dance, Yoga, Parachute Play, Dance Party

Week 4 – Gardens & Growth

Book of the Week: Planting a Rainbow

Circle Time
Greeting Circle, Morning Meeting, Calendar & Weather, Sharing Time, Garden Circle

Literacy
Read story, Story Sequencing, Letter G Hunt, Story Retell, Story Response

Math
Counting Flowers, Number Graphing, Measuring Plants, Sorting Seeds, Graphing Flowers

Art
Flower Painting, Garden Craft, Garden Mural, Flower Craft, Rainbow Mural

Sensory
Soil Bin, Water Play, Rice Bin, Sand Tray, Sensory Bottles

Movement
Movement Song, Stretching, Yoga, Parachute Fun, Dance Party

Week 1 – Baby Animals: Monday

Circle Time
Welcome song. Talk about different baby animals and their mothers.

Literacy
Read Are You My Mother? Ask children how the baby bird felt when searching.

Math
Count toy animals or pictures of animals together.

Art
Make animal masks using paper plates and markers.

Sensory
Sand tray with small animal toys hidden inside.

Movement
Sing and move to an animal song, acting out each animal.

Week 1 – Baby Animals: Tuesday

Circle Time
Morning greetings. Discuss nests and homes for baby animals.

Literacy
Story sequencing – retell Are You My Mother? with picture cards.

Math
Match baby animals to their mothers with cards.

Art
Create a nest craft with paper and shredded materials.

Sensory
Water beads with toy ducks or fish inside.

Movement
Play Freeze Dance – move like different animals and freeze when music stops.

Week 1 – Baby Animals: Wednesday

Circle Time
Calendar and weather check. Talk about farm animals and their babies.

Literacy
Letter Hunt – find the letter A for Animals in the classroom.

Math
Count eggs in a basket. Compare numbers (more/less).

Art
Make a farm collage with pictures of baby animals.

Sensory
Playdough animals – roll and shape animal figures.

Movement
Practice yoga poses – cat pose, cow pose, downward dog.

Week 1 – Baby Animals: Thursday

Circle Time
Sharing Time – children share what pets or animals they know.

Literacy
Story retell – act out parts of Are You My Mother? with puppets.

Math
Graph favorite animals from the class.

Art
Paint or color pictures of baby animals with their mothers.

Sensory
Rice bin with animal figurines to dig for.

Movement
Parachute play – pretend to be baby birds flying from the nest.

Week 1 – Baby Animals: Friday

Circle Time
Animal Circle – review baby animals we learned about.

Literacy
Story response – children draw their favorite part of Are You My Mother?.

Math
Sort animals by type (farm, zoo, pets).

Art
Make animal masks or puppets to take home.

Sensory
Sensory bottles filled with feathers, toy animals, and glitter.

Movement
Dance party – move like animals while music plays.

Week 2 – Easter & Springtime: Monday

Circle Time
Greeting Circle – talk about Easter traditions and springtime.

Literacy
Read The Easter Egg. Discuss the main character's adventure decorating eggs.

Math
Count plastic eggs together. Practice simple addition and subtraction with them.

Art
Decorate paper eggs using crayons, stickers, and glitter.

Sensory
Cotton balls in a bin as 'bunny tails' to explore.

Movement
Sing a spring movement song – hop like bunnies, flap like chicks.

Week 2 – Easter & Springtime: Tuesday

Circle Time
Morning meeting – discuss why we celebrate spring and Easter.

Literacy
Story sequencing – put The Easter Egg story in order with picture cards.

Math
Make repeating egg color patterns (red-blue-red-blue).

Art
Make Easter baskets with construction paper and ribbon handles.

Sensory
Shaving cream play – swirl in food coloring to decorate pretend eggs.

Movement
Stretching – act like waking flowers stretching up toward the sun.

Week 2 – Easter & Springtime: Wednesday

Circle Time
Weather chart – talk about how spring weather helps plants grow.

Literacy
Letter Hunt – find the letter E for Easter in the classroom.

Math
Sort eggs by color and size. Count how many of each group.

Art
Create an egg mural together as a class.

Sensory
Sensory bin filled with plastic eggs and rice to scoop and pour.

Movement
Practice yoga poses – bunny pose (child's pose), egg pose (curl small).

Week 2 – Easter & Springtime: Thursday

Circle Time
Calendar time – talk about baby animals in spring (bunnies, chicks, lambs).

Literacy
Story retell – children act out parts of The Easter Egg.

Math
Count and graph how many bunnies, chicks, and eggs are in pictures.

Art
Make bunny crafts with cotton balls and paper plates.

Sensory
Water play – float plastic eggs in water tables.

Movement
Parachute fun – bounce lightweight eggs or cotton balls on the parachute.

Week 2 – Easter & Springtime: Friday

Circle Time
Sharing Time – children share their favorite part of Easter or spring.

Literacy
Story response – draw a picture of their favorite decorated egg.

Math
Graph egg colors from an egg hunt activity.

Art
Create spring art with flowers, eggs, and rainbows.

Sensory
Sensory bottles with small eggs, glitter, and water.

Movement
Dance party – hop, flap, and move to spring music.

Week 3 – Earth Day & Nature: Monday

Circle Time
Welcome Circle – talk about Earth Day and why we care for our planet.

Literacy
Read The Earth Book. Ask children how they can help the Earth.

Math
Count trees or leaves in pictures. Practice simple addition with them.

Art
Make an Earth collage with blue and green paper scraps.

Sensory
Sand tray with small rocks, sticks, and leaves to explore.

Movement
Go on a nature walk outside or around the classroom.

Week 3 – Earth Day & Nature: Tuesday

Circle Time
Morning meeting – discuss recycling and why it is important.

Literacy
Story sequencing – retell The Earth Book with picture cards.

Math
Number hunt – find numbers hidden in recycled materials.

Art
Make recycle crafts with bottles, paper, or cardboard.

Sensory
Water beads in blue and green for Earth colors.

Movement
Play Freeze Dance pretending to be trees swaying in the wind.

Week 3 – Earth Day & Nature: Wednesday

Circle Time
Calendar and weather – talk about how weather affects the Earth.

Literacy
Letter Hunt – find the letter E for Earth in the classroom.

Math
Sort trash vs. recycling items with pictures or bins.

Art
Create a big Earth mural as a class.

Sensory
Playdough Earth – roll blue and green balls for the planet.

Movement
Practice yoga poses – mountain pose, tree pose.

Week 3 – Earth Day & Nature: Thursday

Circle Time
Sharing Time – children share ways they help the Earth.

Literacy
Story retell – children act out ways to help the Earth from the book.

Math
Graph recycling vs. trash from a classroom activity.

Art
Make nature crafts with leaves, twigs, or paper flowers.

Sensory
Rice bin with toy animals and plants to care for.

Movement
Parachute play – pretend the parachute is the Earth we keep safe.

Week 3 – Earth Day & Nature: Friday

Circle Time
Earth Circle – review what we learned about helping the planet.

Literacy
Story response – children draw their favorite way to help the Earth.

Math
Count and compare plants or trees in classroom pictures.

Art
Make Earth art with paints and glitter.

Sensory
Sensory bottles with blue/green water and glitter.

Movement
Dance party – move like animals that live on Earth.

Week 4 – Gardens & Growth: Monday

Circle Time
Greeting Circle – talk about gardens and how flowers grow.

Literacy
Read Planting a Rainbow. Discuss the flowers in the story.

Math
Count flower pictures or toys. Practice matching numbers to sets.

Art
Paint flowers with bright spring colors.

Sensory
Soil bin with toy flowers and gardening tools.

Movement
Sing and act out 'I'm a Little Flower' – grow tall toward the sun.

Week 4 – Gardens & Growth: Tuesday

Circle Time
Morning meeting – discuss what plants need (water, sun, soil).

Literacy
Story sequencing – retell Planting a Rainbow with cards.

Math
Graph how many children like different types of flowers.

Art
Make garden crafts with construction paper and glue.

Sensory
Water play – pretend to water plants with cups and watering cans.

Movement
Stretching – act out seeds sprouting and flowers blooming.

Week 4 – Gardens & Growth: Wednesday

Circle Time
Calendar and weather – talk about how weather helps plants grow.

Literacy
Letter Hunt – find the letter G for Garden in the classroom.

Math
Measure pretend flowers with rulers or blocks.

Art
Create a class garden mural with paint and paper flowers.

Sensory
Rice bin with hidden seeds and flower cutouts.

Movement
Practice yoga poses – tree pose, flower pose.

Week 4 – Gardens & Growth: Thursday

Circle Time
Sharing Time – children share what gardens they've seen or helped with.

Literacy
Story retell – children act out planting a rainbow of flowers.

Math
Sort seeds by type or size (sunflower, bean, corn).

Art
Make flower crafts with tissue paper petals.

Sensory
Sand tray – bury and dig for seed cutouts.

Movement
Parachute play – pretend the parachute is the sun shining on the flowers.

Week 4 – Gardens & Growth: Friday

Circle Time
Garden Circle – review what we learned about flowers and gardens.

Literacy
Story response – draw their favorite flower from Planting a Rainbow.

Math
Count flowers and create simple patterns (red-yellow-red-yellow).

Art
Make a rainbow mural filled with flowers of many colors.

Sensory
Sensory bottles with seeds, water, and glitter.

Movement
Dance party – move like flowers swaying in the breeze.

Week 1 – Baby Animals

Book of the Week: Are You My Mother?

What baby animal do you like?

Name: _____

Week 2 – Easter & Springtime

Book of the Week: The Easter Egg

How would you decorate your Easter egg?

Name: _____

Week 3 – Earth Day & Nature

Book of the Week: The Earth Book

What can you do to help the Earth?

Name: _____

Week 4 – Gardens & Growth

Book of the Week: Planting a Rainbow

What is your favorite flower to plant?

Name: _____

The Nurtured Path – April Preschool Newsletter

April is full of growth and new beginnings! This month we will explore baby animals, Easter traditions, how to care for the Earth, and the joy of planting a rainbow of flowers. Children will engage in hands-on activities that celebrate spring and encourage curiosity, creativity, and care for nature.

This Month's Themes & Books

- Week 1 – Baby Animals: Are You My Mother?
- Week 2 – Easter & Springtime: The Easter Egg
- Week 3 – Earth Day & Nature: The Earth Book
- Week 4 – Gardens & Growth: Planting a Rainbow

Classroom Highlights

- Learning about baby animals and their mothers • Decorating Easter eggs and creating spring art • Making recycle crafts and celebrating Earth Day • Planting seeds and creating a class garden mural • Enjoying sensory play with soil, water, and flowers

Important Reminders

- Please bring jackets for outdoor play as spring weather can change quickly. • April 22 – Earth Day Celebration (send children in green shirts if possible). • Gardening week – please send any extra seeds, soil, or small pots if you can. • Be mindful of spring allergies and let us know if your child needs accommodations.

Looking Ahead to May

In May, we will learn about butterflies, celebrate Mother's Day, and explore spring weather changes. It will be a month filled with love, growth, and new discoveries!

Thank you for being part of The Nurtured Path family. We look forward to another joyful month of learning together!

May Preschool Curriculum

The Nurtured Path

- Blooming with Learning in May

Week 1 – Butterflies & Insects

Book: The Very Hungry Caterpillar

Monday	Welcome Circle	Read story	Counting caterpillars	Butterfly craft	Sand tray	Butterfly song
Tuesday	Morning Meeting	Story sequencing	Number match	Caterpillar craft	Water beads	Caterpillar crawl
Wednesday	Calendar & Weather	Letter C hunt	Counting butterflies	Insect collage	Playdough insects	Yoga
Thursday	Sharing Time	Story retell	Graph insects	Bug art	Rice bin	Parachute play

Friday	Insect Circle	Story response	Sorting insects	Butterfly wings	Sensory bottles	Dance party

Week 2 – Mother's Day & Families

Book: I Love You Because You're You

Monday	Greeting Circle	Read story	Counting hearts	Heart craft	Cotton balls	Family song
Tuesday	Morning Meeting	Story retell	Heart patterns	Mother's Day card	Shaving cream hearts	Stretching
Wednesday	Weather Chart	Letter M hunt	Sorting families	Family mural	Sensory bin	Yoga

Thursday	Calendar Time	Story sequencing	Counting flowers	Flower craft	Water play	Parachute fun
Friday	Sharing Time	Story response	Graph family activities	Spring art	Sensory bottles	Dance party

Week 3 – Weather & Rain

Book: Come On, Rain!

Monday	Welcome Circle	Read story	Counting raindrops	Raindrop art	Sand tray	Rain dance
Tuesday	Morning Meeting	Story sequencing	Number match	Umbrella craft	Water beads	Freeze dance

Wednesday	Calendar & Weather	Letter R hunt	Sorting weather cards	Weather mural	Playdough clouds	Yoga
Thursday	Sharing Time	Story retell	Graph weather types	Storm art	Rice bin	Parachute play
Friday	Weather Circle	Story response	Counting umbrellas	Rainbow mural	Sensory bottles	Dance party

Week 4 – Friendship & Kindness

Book: Rainbow Fish

Monday	Greeting Circle	Read story	Counting scales	Fish craft	Water play	Friendship song

Tuesday	Morning Meeting	Story retell	Scale patterns	Friendship card	Shaving cream fish	Stretching
Wednesday	Weather Chart	Letter F hunt	Sorting fish	Ocean mural	Sensory bin	Yoga
Thursday	Calendar Time	Story sequencing	Counting fish	Fish craft	Rice bin	Parachute fun
Friday	Sharing Time	Story response	Graph ocean animals	Friendship art	Sensory bottles	Dance party

Week 1 – Butterflies & Insects

Book of the Week: The Very Hungry Caterpillar

Circle Time
Welcome Circle, Morning Meeting, Calendar & Weather, Sharing Time, Insect Circle

Literacy
Read story, Story Sequencing, Letter C Hunt, Story Retell, Story Response

Math
Counting caterpillars, Number Match, Counting butterflies, Graph insects, Sorting insects

Art
Butterfly Craft, Caterpillar Craft, Insect Collage, Bug Art, Butterfly Wings

Sensory
Sand Tray, Water Beads, Playdough Insects, Rice Bin, Sensory Bottles

Movement
Butterfly Song, Caterpillar Crawl, Yoga, Parachute Play, Dance Party

Week 2 – Mother's Day & Families

Book of the Week: I Love You Because You're You

Circle Time
Greeting Circle, Morning Meeting, Weather Chart, Calendar Time, Sharing Time

Literacy
Read story, Story Retell, Letter M Hunt, Story Sequencing, Story Response

Math
Counting hearts, Heart Patterns, Sorting families, Counting flowers, Graph family activities

Art
Heart Craft, Mother's Day Card, Family Mural, Flower Craft, Spring Art

Sensory
Cotton Balls, Shaving Cream Hearts, Sensory Bin, Water Play, Sensory Bottles

Movement
Family Song, Stretching, Yoga, Parachute Fun, Dance Party

Week 3 – Weather & Rain

Book of the Week: Come On, Rain!

Circle Time
Welcome Circle, Morning Meeting, Calendar & Weather, Sharing Time, Weather Circle

Literacy
Read story, Story Sequencing, Letter R Hunt, Story Retell, Story Response

Math
Counting raindrops, Number Match, Sorting weather cards, Graph weather types, Counting umbrellas

Art
Raindrop Art, Umbrella Craft, Weather Mural, Storm Art, Rainbow Mural

Sensory
Sand Tray, Water Beads, Playdough Clouds, Rice Bin, Sensory Bottles

Movement
Rain Dance, Freeze Dance, Yoga, Parachute Play, Dance Party

Week 4 – Friendship & Kindness

Book of the Week: Rainbow Fish

Circle Time
Greeting Circle, Morning Meeting, Weather Chart, Calendar Time, Sharing Time

Literacy
Read story, Story Retell, Letter F Hunt, Story Sequencing, Story Response

Math
Counting Scales, Scale Patterns, Sorting fish, Counting fish, Graph ocean animals

Art
Fish Craft, Friendship Card, Ocean Mural, Fish Craft, Friendship Art

Sensory
Water Play, Shaving Cream Fish, Sensory Bin, Rice Bin, Sensory Bottles

Movement
Friendship Song, Stretching, Yoga, Parachute Fun, Dance Party

Week 1 – Butterflies & Insects: Monday

Circle Time
Welcome song; discuss butterflies and insects.

Literacy
Read The Very Hungry Caterpillar. Discuss first, next, last.

Math
Count caterpillars, sort by size.

Art
Butterfly crafts with paper and paint.

Sensory
Sand tray with toy insects.

Movement
Flap arms like butterflies.

Week 1 – Butterflies & Insects: Tuesday

Circle Time
Morning greetings; discuss caterpillar change.

Literacy
Story sequencing with pictures.

Math
Number matching with caterpillars.

Art
Pom-pom caterpillar crafts.

Sensory
Water beads with toy bugs.

Movement
Crawl like caterpillars, stretch into butterflies.

Week 1 – Butterflies & Insects: Wednesday

Circle Time
Calendar & weather; talk about insects outside.

Literacy
Letter Hunt: C for Caterpillar.

Math
Count butterflies in pictures.

Art
Insect collage with cutouts.

Sensory
Playdough insects.

Movement
Yoga: butterfly pose.

Week 1 – Butterflies & Insects: Thursday

Circle Time
Sharing time about butterflies.

Literacy
Act out the story with props.

Math
Graph insects (beetles, ants, butterflies).

Art
Bug art with paint.

Sensory
Rice bin with toy insects.

Movement
Parachute play as the sky.

Week 1 – Butterflies & Insects: Friday

Circle Time
Review week's learning.

Literacy
Draw favorite part of the story.

Math
Sort insects by type.

Art
Make butterfly wings with tissue.

Sensory
Sensory bottles with insects.

Movement
Dance like insects.

Week 2 – Mother's Day & Families: Monday

Circle Time
Greeting Circle; talk about moms/families.

Literacy
Read I Love You Because You're You.

Math
Count paper hearts.

Art
Heart craft with markers.

Sensory
Cotton ball play.

Movement
Sing family song.

Week 2 – Mother's Day & Families: Tuesday

Circle Time
Share what you love about family.

Literacy
Act out book with puppets.

Math
Heart patterns (red-pink).

Art
Create Mother's Day cards.

Sensory
Shaving cream hearts.

Movement
Stretch like giving hugs.

Week 2 – Mother's Day & Families: Wednesday

Circle Time
Weather chart; discuss family activities.

Literacy
Letter Hunt: M for Mother.

Math
Sort family pictures by size.

Art
Make a family mural.

Sensory
Toy family figures in bin.

Movement
Partner yoga as a family.

Week 2 – Mother's Day & Families: Thursday

Circle Time
Calendar time; discuss Mother's Day.

Literacy
Story sequencing.

Math
Count flowers; make graphs.

Art
Paper flower craft.

Sensory
Water play for flowers.

Movement
Parachute play.

Week 2 – Mother's Day & Families: Friday

Circle Time
Share why you love your family.

Literacy
Draw your family.

Math
Graph favorite family activities.

Art
Spring heart art.

Sensory
Glitter sensory bottles.

Movement
Dance party for family.

Week 3 – Weather & Rain: Monday

Circle Time
Talk about rainy days.

Literacy
Read Come On, Rain!

Math
Count raindrops.

Art
Raindrop art with paint.

Sensory
Sand tray with umbrellas.

Movement
Dance like raindrops.

Week 3 – Weather & Rain: Tuesday

Circle Time
Talk about rain helping plants grow.

Literacy
Sequence story events.

Math
Match numbers to umbrellas.

Art
Umbrella crafts.

Sensory
Water beads as raindrops.

Movement
Freeze dance with thunder sounds.

Week 3 – Weather & Rain: Wednesday

Circle Time
Weather chart.

Literacy
Letter Hunt: R for Rain.

Math
Sort weather cards.

Art
Weather mural.

Sensory
Playdough clouds/raindrops.

Movement
Yoga: rain/cloud/rainbow poses.

Week 3 – Weather & Rain: Thursday

Circle Time
Sharing about rain fun.

Literacy
Act out the story.

Math
Graph favorite weather.

Art
Storm art with cotton clouds.

Sensory
Rice bin weather toys.

Movement
Parachute as stormy sky.

Week 3 – Weather & Rain: Friday

Circle Time
Review weather.

Literacy
Draw favorite part of the book.

Math
Count umbrellas; compare.

Art
Rainbow mural craft.

Sensory
Blue glitter sensory bottles.

Movement
Dance like sunshine.

Week 4 – Friendship & Kindness: Monday

Circle Time
Discuss friends and sharing.

Literacy
Read Rainbow Fish.

Math
Count rainbow scales.

Art
Fish crafts with shiny scales.

Sensory
Water play with toy fish.

Movement
Friendship circle song.

Week 4 – Friendship & Kindness: Tuesday

Circle Time
Talk about good friends.

Literacy
Retell story with puppets.

Math
Make scale patterns.

Art
Make friendship cards.

Sensory
Shaving cream fish.

Movement
Stretch like swimming fish.

Week 4 – Friendship & Kindness: Wednesday

Circle Time
Weather chart/ocean talk.

Literacy
Letter Hunt: F for Fish.

Math
Sort fish by size.

Art
Ocean mural craft.

Sensory
Bin with toy fish/shells.

Movement
Yoga: fish/starfish poses.

Week 4 – Friendship & Kindness: Thursday

Circle Time
Talk about helping/sharing.

Literacy
Sequence Rainbow Fish.

Math
Count fish groups.

Art
Tissue paper fish crafts.

Sensory
Rice bin with shells.

Movement
Parachute as ocean waves.

Week 4 – Friendship & Kindness: Friday

Circle Time
Share about kindness.

Literacy
Draw favorite part of story.

Math
Graph ocean animals.

Art
Friendship rainbow fish art.

Sensory
Glitter fish sensory bottles.

Movement
Dance like fish together.

Week 1 – Butterflies & Insects

Book of the Week: The Very Hungry Caterpillar

What is your favorite food to eat?

Name: _____

Week 2 – Mother's Day & Families

Book of the Week: I Love You Because You're You

Why do you love your family?

Name: _____

Week 3 – Weather & Rain

Book of the Week: Come On, Rain!

What do you like to do on a rainy day?

Name: _____

Week 4 – Friendship & Kindness

Book of the Week: Rainbow Fish

How can you be a good friend?

Name: _____

The Nurtured Path – May Preschool Newsletter

May is a month full of growth, love, and learning! This month we will explore butterflies and insects, celebrate families and Mother's Day, splash into spring weather, and discover the joy of friendship. Children will enjoy creative, hands-on activities that connect learning with real-life experiences.

This Month's Themes & Books

- Week 1 – Butterflies & Insects: The Very Hungry Caterpillar
- Week 2 – Mother's Day & Families: I Love You Because You're You
- Week 3 – Weather & Rain: Come On, Rain!
- Week 4 – Friendship & Kindness: Rainbow Fish

Classroom Highlights

- Watching caterpillars grow and making butterfly crafts • Creating special cards and gifts for Mother's Day • Exploring rain and weather through art and science • Learning about kindness and sharing with Rainbow Fish

Important Reminders

- Mother's Day Celebration – please join us Friday of Week 2! • Bring jackets and boots for rainy weather. • Let us know about any spring allergies or sensitivities. • Encourage children to practice kindness and sharing at home.

Looking Ahead to June

In June, we will enjoy summer fun with themes about oceans, outdoor play, and celebrations. It will be a month full of sunshine, learning, and excitement!

Thank you for being part of The Nurtured Path family. Let's make May a joyful and meaningful month of learning!

June Preschool Curriculum

The Nurtured Path

■■ Jump Into Learning This June
■■

Week 1 – Summer Fun & Play

Book: Jabari Jumps

Monday	Welcome Circle	Read story	Counting jumps	Pool safety art	Water play	Jumping games
Tuesday	Morning Meeting	Story sequencing	Number match	Sun craft	Sand tray	Relay races
Wednesday	Calendar & Weather	Letter J hunt	Measuring jumps	Summer collage	Playdough shapes	Yoga
Thursday	Sharing Time	Story retell	Graph favorite summer activities	Kite craft	Rice bin	Parachute play

Friday	Circle Time	Story response	Sorting summer toys	Beach art	Sensory bottles	Dance party

Week 2 – Ocean Animals

Book: Commotion in the Ocean

Monday	Welcome Circle	Read story	Counting fish	Fish craft	Water beads	Swim movements
Tuesday	Morning Meeting	Story sequencing	Number match	Octopus art	Sand tray	Crab walk
Wednesday	Calendar & Weather	Letter O hunt	Sorting shells	Ocean mural	Playdough sea animals	Yoga

Thursday	Sharing Time	Story retell	Graph ocean animals	Shark craft	Rice bin	Parachute play
Friday	Circle Time	Story response	Counting whales	Sea turtle art	Sensory bottles	Dance party

Week 3 – Camping & Nature

Book: Maisy Goes Camping

Monday	Welcome Circle	Read story	Counting tents	Tent craft	Sand tray	Nature walk
Tuesday	Morning Meeting	Story sequencing	Number match	Campfire art	Leaf rubbings	Stretching

Wednesday	Calendar & Weather	Letter C hunt	Sorting camping gear	Nature collage	Playdough trees	Yoga
Thursday	Sharing Time	Story retell	Graph favorite camping foods	Lantern craft	Rice bin	Parachute play
Friday	Circle Time	Story response	Counting stars	Camping mural	Sensory bottles	Dance party

Week 4 – Community Helpers

Book: Clothesline Clues to Jobs People Do

Monday	Welcome Circle	Read story	Counting tools	Helper hats craft	Sand tray	Pretend play

Tuesday	Morning Meeting	Story sequencing	Number match	Fire truck art	Water play	Marching
Wednesday	Calendar & Weather	Letter H hunt	Sorting uniforms	Community mural	Playdough jobs	Yoga
Thursday	Sharing Time	Story retell	Graph favorite jobs	Doctor bag craft	Rice bin	Parachute play
Friday	Circle Time	Story response	Counting badges	Helper collage	Sensory bottles	Dance party

Week 1 – Summer Fun & Play

Book of the Week: Jabari Jumps

Circle Time
Welcome Circle, Morning Meeting, Calendar & Weather, Sharing Time, Summer Talk

Literacy
Read story, Story Sequencing, Letter J Hunt, Story Retell, Story Response

Math
Counting jumps, Measuring jumps, Sorting summer toys, Graph favorite summer activities, Number Match

Art
Pool Safety Art, Sun Craft, Summer Collage, Kite Craft, Beach Art

Sensory
Water Play, Sand Tray, Playdough Shapes, Rice Bin, Sensory Bottles

Movement
Jumping Games, Relay Races, Yoga, Parachute Play, Dance Party

Week 2 – Ocean Animals

Book of the Week: Commotion in the Ocean

Circle Time
Welcome Circle, Morning Meeting, Calendar & Weather, Sharing Time, Ocean Talk

Literacy
Read story, Story Sequencing, Letter O Hunt, Story Retell, Story Response

Math
Counting Fish, Sorting Shells, Graph ocean animals, Counting whales, Number Match

Art
Fish Craft, Octopus Art, Ocean Mural, Shark Craft, Sea Turtle Art

Sensory
Water Beads, Sand Tray, Playdough Sea Animals, Rice Bin, Sensory Bottles

Movement
Swim Movements, Crab Walk, Yoga, Parachute Play, Dance Party

Week 3 – Camping & Nature

Book of the Week: Maisy Goes Camping

Circle Time
Welcome Circle, Morning Meeting, Calendar & Weather, Sharing Time, Camping Talk

Literacy
Read story, Story Sequencing, Letter C Hunt, Story Retell, Story Response

Math
Counting Tents, Sorting Camping Gear, Graph favorite camping foods, Counting stars, Number Match

Art
Tent Craft, Campfire Art, Nature Collage, Lantern Craft, Camping Mural

Sensory
Sand Tray, Leaf Rubbings, Playdough Trees, Rice Bin, Sensory Bottles

Movement
Nature Walk, Stretching, Yoga, Parachute Play, Dance Party

Week 4 – Community Helpers

Book of the Week: Clothesline Clues to Jobs People Do

Circle Time
Welcome Circle, Morning Meeting, Calendar & Weather, Sharing Time, Helper Talk

Literacy
Read story, Story Sequencing, Letter H Hunt, Story Retell, Story Response

Math
Counting Tools, Sorting Uniforms, Graph favorite jobs, Counting badges, Number Match

Art
Helper Hats Craft, Fire Truck Art, Community Mural, Doctor Bag Craft, Helper Collage

Sensory
Sand Tray, Water Play, Playdough Jobs, Rice Bin, Sensory Bottles

Movement
Pretend Play, Marching, Yoga, Parachute Play, Dance Party

Week 1 – Summer Fun & Play (Jabari Jumps): Monday

Circle Time
Talk about summer fun activities.

Literacy
Read Jabari Jumps. Discuss bravery.

Math
Count jumps together.

Art
Make pool safety posters.

Sensory
Water play with cups and toys.

Movement
Practice jumping safely.

Week 1 – Summer Fun & Play (Jabari Jumps): Tuesday

Circle Time
Share favorite summer activities.

Literacy
Sequence events from the story.

Math
Number matches with pool toys.

Art
Sun crafts with paper and paint.

Sensory
Sand tray with shells.

Movement
Relay races outside.

Week 1 – Summer Fun & Play (Jabari Jumps): Wednesday

Circle Time
Weather chart and summer talk.

Literacy
Letter Hunt: J for Jump.

Math
Measure jumps.

Art
Summer collage with cutouts.

Sensory
Playdough shapes.

Movement
Yoga stretches.

Week 1 – Summer Fun & Play (Jabari Jumps): Thursday

Circle Time
Sharing time: bravery moments.

Literacy
Story retell with props.

Math
Graph favorite summer activities.

Art
Make paper kites.

Sensory
Rice bin with small toys.

Movement
Parachute games.

Week 1 – Summer Fun & Play (Jabari Jumps): Friday

Circle Time
Review what bravery means.

Literacy
Draw favorite part of story.

Math
Sort summer toys.

Art
Beach art with paint.

Sensory
Sensory bottles with glitter.

Movement
Dance party.

Week 2 – Ocean Animals (Commotion in the Ocean): Monday

Circle Time
Talk about ocean animals.

Literacy
Read Commotion in the Ocean.

Math
Count fish in pictures.

Art
Fish crafts.

Sensory
Water beads as ocean.

Movement
Swim movements.

Week 2 – Ocean Animals (Commotion in the Ocean): Tuesday

Circle Time
Discuss sea creatures.

Literacy
Story sequencing with ocean cards.

Math
Number match with shells.

Art
Octopus crafts.

Sensory
Sand tray play.

Movement
Crab walk race.

Week 2 – Ocean Animals (Commotion in the Ocean): Wednesday

Circle Time
Weather chart; ocean weather talk.

Literacy
Letter Hunt: O for Ocean.

Math
Sort shells by size.

Art
Ocean mural.

Sensory
Playdough sea animals.

Movement
Yoga: starfish pose.

Week 2 – Ocean Animals (Commotion in the Ocean): Thursday

Circle Time
Sharing about favorite sea animals.

Literacy
Story retell with props.

Math
Graph favorite ocean animals.

Art
Shark crafts.

Sensory
Rice bin with shells.

Movement
Parachute play as waves.

Week 2 – Ocean Animals (Commotion in the Ocean): Friday

Circle Time
Review sea creatures.

Literacy
Draw favorite sea animal.

Math
Count whales in pictures.

Art
Sea turtle crafts.

Sensory
Ocean sensory bottles.

Movement
Dance like ocean animals.

Week 3 – Camping & Nature (Maisy Goes Camping): Monday

Circle Time

Talk about camping experiences.

Literacy

Read Maisy Goes Camping.

Math

Count tents.

Art

Tent crafts.

Sensory

Sand tray play.

Movement

Nature walk.

Week 3 – Camping & Nature (Maisy Goes Camping): Tuesday

Circle Time

Share favorite outdoor activities.

Literacy

Sequence events from story.

Math

Number matches with camping gear.

Art

Campfire art with tissue paper.

Sensory

Leaf rubbings.

Movement

Stretching outdoors.

Week 3 – Camping & Nature (Maisy Goes Camping): Wednesday

Circle Time
Weather chart & camping gear talk.

Literacy
Letter Hunt: C for Camping.

Math
Sort camping items.

Art
Nature collage.

Sensory
Playdough trees.

Movement
Yoga: tree pose.

Week 3 – Camping & Nature (Maisy Goes Camping): Thursday

Circle Time
Sharing camping stories.

Literacy
Story retell with puppets.

Math
Graph favorite camping foods.

Art
Lantern crafts.

Sensory
Rice bin with stones.

Movement
Parachute fun.

Week 3 – Camping & Nature (Maisy Goes Camping): Friday

Circle Time
Review camping fun.

Literacy
Draw camping experience.

Math
Count stars in pictures.

Art
Camping mural.

Sensory
Sensory bottles with leaves.

Movement
Dance like forest animals.

Week 4 – Community Helpers (Clothesline Clues): Monday

Circle Time
Talk about helpers in the community.

Literacy
Read Clothesline Clues.

Math
Count tools.

Art
Helper hats craft.

Sensory
Sand tray with tools.

Movement
Pretend play as helpers.

Week 4 – Community Helpers (Clothesline Clues): Tuesday

Circle Time
Discuss jobs people do.

Literacy
Sequence jobs from story.

Math
Number match with tools.

Art
Fire truck art.

Sensory
Water play with cups.

Movement
March like firefighters.

Week 4 – Community Helpers (Clothesline Clues): Wednesday

Circle Time
Weather chart; job uniforms talk.

Literacy
Letter Hunt: H for Helpers.

Math
Sort uniforms.

Art
Community mural.

Sensory
Playdough jobs.

Movement
Yoga: strong poses.

Week 4 – Community Helpers (Clothesline Clues): Thursday

Circle Time
Share about helpers children know.

Literacy
Story retell with props.

Math
Graph favorite jobs.

Art
Doctor bag crafts.

Sensory
Rice bin with tools.

Movement
Parachute play.

Week 4 – Community Helpers (Clothesline Clues): Friday

Circle Time
Review helpers and kindness.

Literacy
Draw favorite helper.

Math
Count badges.

Art
Helper collage.

Sensory
Helper sensory bottles.

Movement
Dance party as helpers.

Week 1 – Summer Fun & Play

Book of the Week: Jabari Jumps

What makes you feel brave?

Name: _____

Week 2 – Ocean Animals

Book of the Week: Commotion in the Ocean

What is your favorite ocean animal?

Name: _____

Week 3 – Camping & Nature

Book of the Week: Maisy Goes Camping

What would you bring on a camping trip?

Name: _____

Week 4 – Community Helpers

Book of the Week: Clothesline Clues to Jobs

People Do What do you want to be when

you grow up?

Name: _____

The Nurtured Path – June Preschool Newsletter

June brings summer fun, outdoor play, and exciting themes! This month we will enjoy swimming stories, explore ocean animals, go camping in nature, and learn about community helpers. Children will experience hands-on activities that connect learning to the world around them.

This Month's Themes & Books

- Week 1 – Summer Fun & Play: Jabari Jumps
- Week 2 – Ocean Animals: Commotion in the Ocean
- Week 3 – Camping & Nature: Maisy Goes Camping
- Week 4 – Community Helpers: Clothesline Clues to Jobs People Do

Classroom Highlights

• Pool safety posters and bravery lessons • Ocean crafts and sea creature games • Camping pretend play and campfire crafts • Exploring community helpers with role play

Important Reminders

• Bring hats, sunscreen, and water bottles for outdoor play. • Keep us updated on any summer allergies. • Encourage children to share stories about helpers in their community.

Looking Ahead to July

In July, we will celebrate summer with patriotic themes, outdoor celebrations, and more summer learning fun!

Thank you for being part of The Nurtured Path family. Let's make June full of sunshine and learning!

July Preschool Curriculum

The Nurtured Path

■ Celebrating Learning All July ■

Week 1 – Independence & Community

Book: The Night Before the Fourth of July

Monday	Welcome Circle	Read story	Count stars /stripes	Flag craft	Sand tray	Parade march
Tuesday	Morning Meeting	Story sequencing	Number match	Firework art	Water play	Patriotic dance
Wednesday	Calendar & Weather	Letter J hunt	Sorting red/white/blue	Community mural	Playdough stars	Yoga
Thursday	Sharing Time	Story retell	Graph favorite celebrations	Hat craft	Rice bin	Parachute play

Friday	Circle Time	Story response	Counting fireworks	July collage	Sensory bottles	Dance party

Week 2 – Summer Fruits & Healthy Eating

Book: Eating the Alphabet

Monday	Welcome Circle	Read story	Count apples	Fruit stamping	Fruit bin	Fruit dance
Tuesday	Morning Meeting	Story sequencing	Number match	Banana craft	Sand tray	Stretching
Wednesday	Calendar & Weather	Letter F hunt	Sorting fruits	Fruit salad art	Playdough food	Yoga

Thursday	Sharing Time	Story retell	Graph favorite fruits	Orange craft	Rice bin	Parachute play
Friday	Circle Time	Story response	Counting grapes	Healthy food mural	Sensory bottles	Dance party

Week 3 – Space & Imagination

Book: Roaring Rockets

Monday	Welcome Circle	Read story	Count rockets	Rocket craft	Moon sand	Rocket jumps
Tuesday	Morning Meeting	Story sequencing	Number match	Planet art	Sand tray	Astronaut walk

Wednesday	Calendar & Weather	Letter R hunt	Sorting planets	Space mural	Playdough stars	Yoga
Thursday	Sharing Time	Story retell	Graph favorite planets	Alien craft	Rice bin	Parachute play
Friday	Circle Time	Story response	Counting stars	Galaxy art	Sensory bottles	Dance party

Week 4 – Zoo Animals & Adventures

Book: Put Me in the Zoo

Monday	Welcome Circle	Read story	Count animals	Zoo collage	Animal bin	Animal walks

Tuesday	Morning Meeting	Story sequencing	Number match	Spotty animal craft	Sand tray	Animal stretches
Wednesday	Calendar & Weather	Letter Z hunt	Sorting animals	Zoo mural	Playdough animals	Yoga
Thursday	Sharing Time	Story retell	Graph favorite animals	Mask craft	Rice bin	Parachute play
Friday	Circle Time	Story response	Counting spots	Zoo art	Sensory bottles	Dance party

Week 1 – Independence & Community

Book of the Week: The Night Before the Fourth of July

Circle Time
Welcome Circle, Morning Meeting, Calendar & Weather, Sharing Time, Parade Talk

Literacy
Read story, Story Sequencing, Letter J Hunt, Story Retell, Story Response

Math
Count stars/stripes, Number Match, Sorting red/white/blue, Graph celebrations, Counting fireworks

Art
Flag Craft, Firework Art, Community Mural, Hat Craft, July Collage

Sensory
Sand Tray, Water Play, Playdough Stars, Rice Bin, Sensory Bottles

Movement
Parade March, Patriotic Dance, Yoga, Parachute Play, Dance Party

Week 2 – Summer Fruits & Healthy Eating

Book of the Week: Eating the Alphabet

Circle Time
Welcome Circle, Morning Meeting, Calendar & Weather, Sharing Time, Fruit Talk

Literacy
Read story, Story Sequencing, Letter F Hunt, Story Retell, Story Response

Math
Count Apples, Number Match, Sorting Fruits, Graph favorite fruits, Counting grapes

Art
Fruit Stamping, Banana Craft, Fruit Salad Art, Orange Craft, Healthy Food Mural

Sensory
Fruit Bin, Sand Tray, Playdough Food, Rice Bin, Sensory Bottles

Movement
Fruit Dance, Stretching, Yoga, Parachute Play, Dance Party

Week 3 – Space & Imagination

Book of the Week: Roaring Rockets

Circle Time
Welcome Circle, Morning Meeting, Calendar & Weather, Sharing Time, Space Talk

Literacy
Read story, Story Sequencing, Letter R Hunt, Story Retell, Story Response

Math
Count Rockets, Number Match, Sorting Planets, Graph favorite planets, Counting stars

Art
Rocket Craft, Planet Art, Space Mural, Alien Craft, Galaxy Art

Sensory
Moon Sand, Sand Tray, Playdough Stars, Rice Bin, Sensory Bottles

Movement
Rocket Jumps, Astronaut Walk, Yoga, Parachute Play, Dance Party

Week 4 – Zoo Animals & Adventures

Book of the Week: Put Me in the Zoo

Circle Time
Welcome Circle, Morning Meeting, Calendar & Weather, Sharing Time, Zoo Talk

Literacy
Read story, Story Sequencing, Letter Z Hunt, Story Retell, Story Response

Math
Count Animals, Number Match, Sorting Animals, Graph favorite animals, Counting spots

Art
Zoo Collage, Spotty Animal Craft, Zoo Mural, Mask Craft, Zoo Art

Sensory
Animal Bin, Sand Tray, Playdough Animals, Rice Bin, Sensory Bottles

Movement
Animal Walks, Animal Stretches, Yoga, Parachute Play, Dance Party

Week 1 – Independence & Community (The Night Before the Fourth of July): Monday

Circle Time
Talk about Independence Day.

Literacy
Read The Night Before the Fourth of July.

Math
Count stars and stripes.

Art
Make flags with paper.

Sensory
Sand tray with toy flags.

Movement
March like in a parade.

Week 1 – Independence & Community (The Night Before the Fourth of July): Tuesday

Circle Time
Share favorite celebrations.

Literacy
Sequence events from the story.

Math
Number match with fireworks.

Art
Firework art with paint.

Sensory
Water play with red/blue toys.

Movement
Patriotic dance.

Week 1 – Independence & Community (The Night Before the Fourth of July): Wednesday

Circle Time
Weather chart & July talk.

Literacy
Letter Hunt: J for July.

Math
Sort red/white/blue objects.

Art
Community mural.

Sensory
Playdough stars.

Movement
Yoga star pose.

Week 1 – Independence & Community (The Night Before the Fourth of July): Thursday

Circle Time
Talk about parades.

Literacy
Retell story with props.

Math
Graph favorite celebrations.

Art
Make parade hats.

Sensory
Rice bin with toys.

Movement
Parachute play.

Week 1 – Independence & Community (The Night Before the Fourth of July): Friday

Circle Time
Review July 4th traditions.

Literacy
Draw favorite celebration.

Math
Count fireworks.

Art
July collage.

Sensory
Sensory bottles red/blue.

Movement
Dance party.

Week 2 – Summer Fruits & Healthy Eating (Eating the Alphabet): Monday

Circle Time
Talk about favorite fruits.

Literacy
Read Eating the Alphabet.

Math
Count apples.

Art
Fruit stamping with paint.

Sensory
Fruit bin with toys.

Movement
Fruit dance.

Week 2 – Summer Fruits & Healthy Eating (Eating the Alphabet): Tuesday

Circle Time
Share healthy snacks.

Literacy
Story sequencing with fruit cards.

Math
Number match with bananas.

Art
Banana crafts.

Sensory
Sand tray with food toys.

Movement
Stretching exercises.

Week 2 – Summer Fruits & Healthy Eating (Eating the Alphabet): Wednesday

Circle Time
Weather chart & fruit talk.

Literacy
Letter Hunt: F for Fruit.

Math
Sort fruits by color.

Art
Fruit salad art.

Sensory
Playdough food shapes.

Movement
Yoga fruit poses.

Week 2 – Summer Fruits & Healthy Eating (Eating the Alphabet): Thursday

Circle Time
Talk about farmers' markets.

Literacy
Story retell with props.

Math
Graph favorite fruits.

Art
Orange crafts.

Sensory
Rice bin with food toys.

Movement
Parachute play.

Week 2 – Summer Fruits & Healthy Eating (Eating the Alphabet): Friday

Circle Time
Review healthy eating.

Literacy
Draw favorite fruit.

Math
Count grapes.

Art
Healthy food mural.

Sensory
Fruit sensory bottles.

Movement
Dance party.

Week 3 – Space & Imagination (Roaring Rockets): Monday

Circle Time

Talk about space travel.

Literacy

Read Roaring Rockets.

Math

Count rockets.

Art

Rocket crafts.

Sensory

Moon sand play.

Movement

Rocket jumps.

Week 3 – Space & Imagination (Roaring Rockets): Tuesday

Circle Time
Share favorite planets.

Literacy
Story sequencing with rocket cards.

Math
Number match with stars.

Art
Planet art.

Sensory
Sand tray as moon.

Movement
Astronaut walk.

Week 3 – Space & Imagination (Roaring Rockets): Wednesday

Circle Time

Weather chart & space talk.

Literacy

Letter Hunt: R for Rocket.

Math

Sort planets by size.

Art

Space mural.

Sensory

Playdough stars.

Movement

Yoga star pose.

Week 3 – Space & Imagination (Roaring Rockets): Thursday

Circle Time
Talk about astronauts.

Literacy
Story retell with props.

Math
Graph favorite planets.

Art
Alien crafts.

Sensory
Rice bin with stars.

Movement
Parachute space play.

Week 3 – Space & Imagination (Roaring Rockets): Friday

Circle Time
Review planets.

Literacy
Draw favorite rocket/planet.

Math
Count stars.

Art
Galaxy art.

Sensory
Space sensory bottles.

Movement
Dance like astronauts.

Week 4 – Zoo Animals & Adventures (Put Me in the Zoo): Monday

Circle Time

Talk about zoo trips.

Literacy

Read Put Me in the Zoo.

Math

Count animals.

Art

Zoo collage.

Sensory

Animal bin play.

Movement

Walk like zoo animals.

Week 4 – Zoo Animals & Adventures (Put Me in the Zoo): Tuesday

Circle Time
Share favorite animals.

Literacy
Story sequencing with animal cards.

Math
Number match with animals.

Art
Spotty animal crafts.

Sensory
Sand tray animal play.

Movement
Animal stretches.

Week 4 – Zoo Animals & Adventures (Put Me in the Zoo): Wednesday

Circle Time
Weather chart & animal talk.

Literacy
Letter Hunt: Z for Zoo.

Math
Sort animals by type.

Art
Zoo mural.

Sensory
Playdough animals.

Movement
Yoga animal poses.

Week 4 – Zoo Animals & Adventures (Put Me in the Zoo): Thursday

Circle Time
Talk about zoo adventures.

Literacy
Story retell with props.

Math
Graph favorite animals.

Art
Animal mask crafts.

Sensory
Rice bin with animal toys.

Movement
Parachute play.

Week 4 – Zoo Animals & Adventures (Put Me in the Zoo): Friday

Circle Time
Review zoo animals.

Literacy
Draw favorite animal.

Math
Count animal spots.

Art
Zoo art with paint.

Sensory
Animal sensory bottles.

Movement
Dance party as animals.

Week 1 – Independence & Community

Book of the Week: The Night Before the Fourth of July

What do you like to do on the Fourth of July?

Name: _____

Week 2 – Summer Fruits & Healthy Eating

Book of the Week: Eating the Alphabet

What is your favorite fruit or vegetable?

Name: _____

Week 3 – Space & Imagination

Book of the Week: Roaring Rockets

What would you like to see in space?

Name: _____

Week 4 – Zoo Animals & Adventures

Book of the Week: Put Me in the Zoo

What is your favorite zoo animal?

Name: _____

The Nurtured Path – July Preschool Newsletter

July is packed with celebration and discovery! This month we will explore the excitement of Independence Day, enjoy learning about fruits and healthy eating, blast off into space adventures, and finish the month with zoo animal fun. Children will build creativity, knowledge, and teamwork through engaging activities.

This Month's Themes & Books

• Week 1 – Independence & Community: The Night Before the Fourth of July
• Week 2 – Summer Fruits & Healthy Eating: Eating the Alphabet
• Week 3 – Space & Imagination: Roaring Rockets
• Week 4 – Zoo Animals & Adventures: Put Me in the Zoo

Classroom Highlights

• Flag crafts and firework art • Fruit stamping and healthy eating games • Rocket jumps and space murals • Zoo collages and animal walks

Important Reminders

• Please send hats, sunscreen, and water bottles for hot summer days. • Pack healthy snacks to go along with our nutrition theme. • Watch for classroom notes about field trips or special zoo activities.

Looking Ahead to August

In August, we will prepare for back-to-school routines with themes on friendship, new classrooms, and fresh starts. Exciting activities will help ease the transition into the new school year.

Thank you for being part of The Nurtured Path family. Let's make July bright, fun, and full of learning!

August Preschool
Curriculum The Nurtured Path

■ Back to School, Back to Fun! ■

Week 1 – Back to School & Feelings

Book: The Kissing Hand

Monday	Welcome Circle	Read story	Counting friends	Handprint craft	Sand tray	Feelings song
Tuesday	Morning Meeting	Story sequencing	Number match	Heart craft	Playdough hands	Movement game
Wednesday	Calendar & Weather	Letter K hunt	Sorting emotions	Chester raccoon craft	Rice bin	Yoga
Thursday	Sharing Time	Story retell	Graph feelings	Friendship collage	Water play	Parachute play

Friday	Circle Time	Story response	Counting hearts	Feelings mural	Sensory bottles	Dance party

Week 2 – All About Me & Family

Book: I Like Myself!

Monday	Welcome Circle	Read story	Count family members	Self-portrait art	Family bin	Movement game
Tuesday	Morning Meeting	Story sequencing	Number match	Family tree craft	Sand tray	Stretching
Wednesday	Calendar & Weather	Letter M hunt	Sorting family photos	Collage of me	Playdough faces	Yoga

Thursday	Sharing Time	Story retell	Graph family sizes	All About Me poster	Rice bin	Parachute play
Friday	Circle Time	Story response	Counting siblings	Family mural	Sensory bottles	Dance party

Week 3 – Friendship & Sharing

Book: Should I Share My Ice Cream?

Monday	Welcome Circle	Read story	Counting cones	Ice cream craft	Sand tray	Sharing game
Tuesday	Morning Meeting	Story sequencing	Number match	Friendship bracelets	Water play	Stretching

Wednesday	Calendar & Weather	Letter I hunt	Sorting colors of cones	Friendship collage	Playdough cones	Yoga
Thursday	Sharing Time	Story retell	Graph favorite ice cream	Cone craft	Rice bin	Parachute play
Friday	Circle Time	Story response	Counting scoops	Friendship mural	Sensory bottles	Dance party

Week 4 – Community Helpers

Book: Whose Hat Is This?

Monday	Welcome Circle	Read story	Counting hats	Hat craft	Sand tray	Pretend play

Day							
Tuesday	Morning Meeting	Story sequencing	Number match	Fire hat art	Water play	Marching	
Wednesday	Calendar & Weather	Letter H hunt	Sorting jobs	Community mural	Playdough hats	Yoga	
Thursday	Sharing Time	Story retell	Graph favorite jobs	Helper tools collage	Rice bin	Parachute play	
Friday	Circle Time	Story response	Counting badges	Helper mural	Sensory bottles	Dance party	

Week 1 – Back to School & Feelings

Book of the Week: The Kissing Hand

Circle Time
Welcome Circle, Morning Meeting, Calendar & Weather, Sharing Time, Feelings Talk

Literacy
Read story, Story Sequencing, Letter K Hunt, Story Retell, Story Response

Math
Counting friends, Number Match, Sorting emotions, Graph feelings, Counting hearts

Art
Handprint Craft, Heart Craft, Chester Raccoon Craft, Friendship Collage, Feelings Mural

Sensory
Sand Tray, Playdough Hands, Rice Bin, Water Play, Sensory Bottles

Movement
Feelings Song, Movement Game, Yoga, Parachute Play, Dance Party

Week 2 – All About Me & Family

Book of the Week: I Like Myself!

Circle Time
Welcome Circle, Morning Meeting, Calendar & Weather, Sharing Time, Family Talk

Literacy
Read story, Story Sequencing, Letter M Hunt, Story Retell, Story Response

Math
Counting family members, Number Match, Sorting family photos, Graph family sizes, Counting siblings

Art
Self-Portrait Art, Family Tree Craft, Collage of Me, All About Me Poster, Family Mural

Sensory
Family Bin, Sand Tray, Playdough Faces, Rice Bin, Sensory Bottles

Movement
Movement Game, Stretching, Yoga, Parachute Play, Dance Party

Week 3 – Friendship & Sharing

Book of the Week: Should I Share My Ice Cream?

Circle Time
Welcome Circle, Morning Meeting, Calendar & Weather, Sharing Time, Friendship Talk

Literacy
Read story, Story Sequencing, Letter I Hunt, Story Retell, Story Response

Math
Counting cones, Number Match, Sorting colors of cones, Graph favorite ice cream, Counting scoops

Art
Ice Cream Craft, Friendship Bracelets, Friendship Collage, Cone Craft, Friendship Mural

Sensory
Sand Tray, Water Play, Playdough Cones, Rice Bin, Sensory Bottles

Movement
Sharing Game, Stretching, Yoga, Parachute Play, Dance Party

Week 4 – Community Helpers

Book of the Week: Whose Hat Is This?

Circle Time
Welcome Circle, Morning Meeting, Calendar & Weather, Sharing Time, Job Talk

Literacy
Read story, Story Sequencing, Letter H Hunt, Story Retell, Story Response

Math
Counting hats, Number Match, Sorting jobs, Graph favorite jobs, Counting badges

Art
Hat Craft, Fire Hat Art, Community Mural, Helper Tools Collage, Helper Mural

Sensory
Sand Tray, Water Play, Playdough Hats, Rice Bin, Sensory Bottles

Movement
Pretend Play, Marching, Yoga, Parachute Play, Dance Party

Week 1 – Back to School & Feelings (The Kissing Hand): Monday

Circle Time
Discuss first day feelings.

Literacy
Read The Kissing Hand.

Math
Count new friends.

Art
Handprint crafts.

Sensory
Sand tray play.

Movement
Feelings song and dance.

Week 1 – Back to School & Feelings (The Kissing Hand): Tuesday

Circle Time
Share feelings about school.

Literacy
Story sequencing activity.

Math
Number match with hearts.

Art
Heart crafts.

Sensory
Playdough hands.

Movement
Movement game: Find a friend.

Week 1 – Back to School & Feelings (The Kissing Hand): Wednesday

Circle Time
Weather chart & feelings talk.

Literacy
Letter Hunt: K for Kissing Hand.

Math
Sort emotion cards.

Art
Chester raccoon craft.

Sensory
Rice bin with toys.

Movement
Yoga calming poses.

Week 1 – Back to School & Feelings (The Kissing Hand): Thursday

Circle Time
Talk about bravery.

Literacy
Retell story with puppets.

Math
Graph how we feel today.

Art
Friendship collage.

Sensory
Water play.

Movement
Parachute play.

Week 1 – Back to School & Feelings (The Kissing Hand): Friday

Circle Time
Review our week.

Literacy
Draw favorite story part.

Math
Count hearts on chart.

Art
Feelings mural.

Sensory
Glitter sensory bottles.

Movement
Dance party.

Week 2 – All About Me & Family (I Like Myself!): Monday

Circle Time
Talk about what makes us special.

Literacy
Read I Like Myself!

Math
Count family members.

Art
Self-portrait art.

Sensory
Family bin play.

Movement
Movement game: Show your style.

Week 2 – All About Me & Family (I Like Myself!): Tuesday

Circle Time
Share family stories.

Literacy
Story sequencing activity.

Math
Number match with family photos.

Art
Family tree craft.

Sensory
Sand tray with toy people.

Movement
Stretching exercises.

Week 2 – All About Me & Family (I Like Myself!): Wednesday

Circle Time
Weather chart & talk about me.

Literacy
Letter Hunt: M for Myself.

Math
Sort family pictures.

Art
Collage of me.

Sensory
Playdough faces.

Movement
Yoga: proud poses.

Week 2 – All About Me & Family (I Like Myself!): Thursday

Circle Time
Talk about families.

Literacy
Retell story with props.

Math
Graph family sizes.

Art
All About Me poster.

Sensory
Rice bin play.

Movement
Parachute play.

Week 2 – All About Me & Family (I Like Myself!): Friday

Circle Time
Review our week.

Literacy
Draw favorite family activity.

Math
Count siblings.

Art
Family mural.

Sensory
Family sensory bottles.

Movement
Dance party.

Week 3 – Friendship & Sharing (Should I Share My Ice Cream?): Monday

Circle Time
Talk about what friends do.

Literacy
Read Should I Share My Ice Cream?.

Math
Count ice cream cones.

Art
Ice cream crafts.

Sensory
Sand tray with scoops.

Movement
Sharing game.

Week 3 – Friendship & Sharing (Should I Share My Ice Cream?): Tuesday

Circle Time
Share about friends.

Literacy
Story sequencing activity.

Math
Number match with cones.

Art
Make friendship bracelets.

Sensory
Water play with scoops.

Movement
Stretching together.

Week 3 – Friendship & Sharing (Should I Share My Ice Cream?): Wednesday

Circle Time
Weather chart & talk about friends.

Literacy
Letter Hunt: I for Ice Cream.

Math
Sort cones by color.

Art
Friendship collage.

Sensory
Playdough cones.

Movement
Yoga partner poses.

Week 3 – Friendship & Sharing (Should I Share My Ice Cream?): Thursday

Circle Time
Talk about sharing.

Literacy
Retell story with puppets.

Math
Graph favorite ice cream.

Art
Cone crafts.

Sensory
Rice bin with cones.

Movement
Parachute play.

Week 3 – Friendship & Sharing (Should I Share My Ice Cream?): Friday

Circle Time
Review sharing week.

Literacy
Draw favorite ice cream.

Math
Count scoops on chart.

Art
Friendship mural.

Sensory
Ice cream sensory bottles.

Movement
Dance party.

Week 4 – Community Helpers (Whose Hat Is This?): Monday

Circle Time

Talk about helpers in our community.

Literacy

Read Whose Hat Is This?.

Math

Count hats.

Art

Hat crafts.

Sensory

Sand tray with hats.

Movement

Pretend play as helpers.

Week 4 – Community Helpers (Whose Hat Is This?): Tuesday

Circle Time
Share about helpers we know.

Literacy
Story sequencing activity.

Math
Number match with tools.

Art
Fire hat crafts.

Sensory
Water play.

Movement
March like helpers.

Week 4 – Community Helpers (Whose Hat Is This?): Wednesday

Circle Time
Weather chart & helpers talk.

Literacy
Letter Hunt: H for Hat.

Math
Sort jobs by hat.

Art
Community mural.

Sensory
Playdough hats.

Movement
Yoga strong poses.

Week 4 – Community Helpers (Whose Hat Is This?): Thursday

Circle Time
Talk about what helpers do.

Literacy
Retell story with props.

Math
Graph favorite jobs.

Art
Helper tools collage.

Sensory
Rice bin with hats.

Movement
Parachute play.

Week 4 – Community Helpers (Whose Hat Is This?): Friday

Circle Time
Review helpers week.

Literacy
Draw favorite helper.

Math
Count badges.

Art
Helper mural.

Sensory
Helper sensory bottles.

Movement
Dance party.

Week 1 – Back to School & Feelings

Book of the Week: The Kissing Hand

What makes you feel brave at school?

Name: _____

Week 2 – All About Me & Family

Book of the Week: I Like Myself!

What do you like most about yourself?

Name: _____

Week 3 – Friendship & Sharing

Book of the Week: Should I Share My Ice Cream?

What is something you can share with a friend?

Name: _____

Week 4 – Community Helpers

Book of the Week: Whose Hat Is This?

What job would you like to do when you grow up?

Name: _____

The Nurtured Path – August Preschool Newsletter

Welcome to a brand-new school year! August is all about building routines, learning about ourselves, and making new friends. This month we will read heartwarming stories, celebrate self-confidence, practice sharing, and explore the jobs of community helpers.

This Month's Themes & Books

• Week 1 – Back to School & Feelings: The Kissing Hand

• Week 2 – All About Me & Family: I Like Myself!

• Week 3 – Friendship & Sharing: Should I Share My Ice Cream?

• Week 4 – Community Helpers: Whose Hat Is This?

Classroom Highlights

• Handprint crafts and bravery lessons • Self-portraits and family trees • Friendship bracelets and sharing games • Helper hats and community murals

Important Reminders

• Please send in family photos for our All About Me projects. • Make sure your child has a labeled water bottle and supplies. • Help us practice daily routines by arriving on time.

Looking Ahead to September

In September, we will explore the five senses, apples, fall weather, and friendship. Exciting activities will guide us into the new season of learning.

Thank you for being part of The Nurtured Path family. We are excited to start this school year together!

September Preschool Curriculum

The Nurtured Path

■ Falling Into Learning ■

Week 1 – Back to School Rules

Book: David Goes to School

Monday	Welcome Circle	Read story	Counting school items	School rules chart	Sand tray	School walk
Tuesday	Morning Meeting	Story sequencing	Number match	Name craft	Playdough letters	Stretching
Wednesday	Calendar & Weather	Letter D hunt	Sorting supplies	School collage	Rice bin	Yoga
Thursday	Sharing Time	Story retell	Graph rules we follow	School poster	Water play	Parachute play

Friday	Circle Time	Story response	Counting friends	School mural	Sensory bottles	Dance party

Week 2 – My Five Senses

Book: My Five Senses

Monday	Welcome Circle	Read story	Count senses	Sense collage	Sand tray	Movement game
Tuesday	Morning Meeting	Story sequencing	Number match	Taste test art	Playdough noses	Stretching
Wednesday	Calendar & Weather	Letter S hunt	Sorting senses	Texture craft	Rice bin	Yoga

Thursday	Sharing Time	Story retell	Graph favorite senses	Sound shakers	Water play	Parachute play
Friday	Circle Time	Story response	Counting body parts	Senses mural	Sensory bottles	Dance party

Week 3 – Friendship & Sharing

Book: Should I Share My Ice Cream?

Monday	Welcome Circle	Read story	Counting cones	Ice cream craft	Sand tray	Sharing game
Tuesday	Morning Meeting	Story sequencing	Number match	Friendship bracelets	Water play	Stretching

Wednesday	Calendar & Weather	Letter I hunt	Sorting colors of cones	Friendship collage	Playdough cones	Yoga
Thursday	Sharing Time	Story retell	Graph favorite ice cream	Cone craft	Rice bin	Parachute play
Friday	Circle Time	Story response	Counting scoops	Friendship mural	Sensory bottles	Dance party

Week 4 – Apples & Fall Weather

Book: Apple Trouble

Monday	Welcome Circle	Read story	Counting apples	Apple craft	Sand tray	Apple walk

Tuesday	Morning Meeting	Story sequencing	Number match	Apple prints	Playdough apples	Stretching
Wednesday	Calendar & Weather	Letter A hunt	Sorting apples	Apple collage	Rice bin	Yoga
Thursday	Sharing Time	Story retell	Graph apple colors	Fall leaf craft	Water play	Parachute play
Friday	Circle Time	Story response	Counting leaves	Fall mural	Sensory bottles	Dance party

Week 1 – Back to School Rules

Book of the Week: David Goes to School

Circle Time
Welcome Circle, Morning Meeting, Calendar & Weather, Sharing Time, Rules Talk

Literacy
Read story, Story Sequencing, Letter D Hunt, Story Retell, Story Response

Math
Counting school items, Number Match, Sorting supplies, Graph rules, Counting friends

Art
School Rules Chart, Name Craft, School Collage, Poster Making, School Mural

Sensory
Sand Tray, Playdough Letters, Rice Bin, Water Play, Sensory Bottles

Movement
School Walk, Stretching, Yoga, Parachute Play, Dance Party

Week 2 – My Five Senses

Book of the Week: My Five Senses

Circle Time
Welcome Circle, Morning Meeting, Calendar & Weather, Sharing Time, Sense Talk

Literacy
Read story, Story Sequencing, Letter S Hunt, Story Retell, Story Response

Math
Counting senses, Number Match, Sorting sense items, Graph favorite sense, Counting body parts

Art
Sense Collage, Taste Test Art, Texture Craft, Sound Shakers, Senses Mural

Sensory
Sand Tray, Playdough Noses, Rice Bin, Water Play, Sensory Bottles

Movement
Movement Game, Stretching, Yoga, Parachute Play, Dance Party

Week 3 – Friendship & Sharing

Book of the Week: Should I Share My Ice Cream?

Circle Time
Welcome Circle, Morning Meeting, Calendar & Weather, Sharing Time, Friendship Talk

Literacy
Read story, Story Sequencing, Letter I Hunt, Story Retell, Story Response

Math
Counting cones, Number Match, Sorting cones by color, Graph favorite ice cream, Counting scoops

Art
Ice Cream Craft, Friendship Bracelets, Friendship Collage, Cone Craft, Friendship Mural

Sensory
Sand Tray, Water Play, Playdough Cones, Rice Bin, Sensory Bottles

Movement
Sharing Game, Stretching, Yoga, Parachute Play, Dance Party

Week 4 – Apples & Fall Weather

Book of the Week: Apple Trouble

Circle Time
Welcome Circle, Morning Meeting, Calendar & Weather, Sharing Time, Apple Talk

Literacy
Read story, Story Sequencing, Letter A Hunt, Story Retell, Story Response

Math
Counting apples, Number Match, Sorting apples, Graph apple colors, Counting leaves

Art
Apple Craft, Apple Prints, Apple Collage, Fall Leaf Craft, Fall Mural

Sensory
Sand Tray, Playdough Apples, Rice Bin, Water Play, Sensory Bottles

Movement
Apple Walk, Stretching, Yoga, Parachute Play, Dance Party

Week 1 – Back to School Rules (David Goes to School): Monday

Circle Time
Discuss school rules and why they are important.

Literacy
Read David Goes to School.

Math
Count school items in the classroom.

Art
Make a school rules chart.

Sensory
Sand tray with letter cards.

Movement
Walk around school identifying rules.

Week 1 – Back to School Rules (David Goes to School): Tuesday

Circle Time
Talk about good choices.

Literacy
Story sequencing activity.

Math
Number match with supplies.

Art
Name crafts with letters.

Sensory
Playdough letters.

Movement
Stretching exercises

Week 1 – Back to School Rules (David Goes to School): Wednesday

Circle Time
Weather chart & talk about respect.

Literacy
Letter Hunt: D for David.

Math
Sort supplies by type.

Art
School collage.

Sensory
Rice bin with letters.

Movement
Yoga calm poses.

Week 1 – Back to School Rules (David Goes to School): Thursday

Circle Time
Share favorite school rules.

Literacy
Retell story with props.

Math
Graph rules we follow.

Art
Make a poster of rules.

Sensory
Water play.

Movement
Parachute play.

Week 1 – Back to School Rules (David Goes to School): Friday

Circle Time
Review rules we learned.

Literacy
Draw favorite story part.

Math
Count classroom friends.

Art
Make a mural about rules.

Sensory
Sensory bottles.

Movement
Dance party

Week 2 – My Five Senses (My Five Senses): Monday

Circle Time
Introduce five senses.

Literacy
Read My Five Senses.

Math
Count five senses.

Art
Make a senses collage.

Sensory
Sand tray play.

Movement
Movement game: act out senses.

Week 2 – My Five Senses (My Five Senses): Tuesday

Circle Time
Talk about taste.

Literacy
Story sequencing activity.

Math
Number match with senses cards.

Art
Taste test art project.

Sensory
Playdough noses.

Movement
Stretching exercises.

Week 2 – My Five Senses (My Five Senses): Wednesday

Circle Time
Weather chart & sense talk.

Literacy
Letter Hunt: S for Senses.

Math
Sort items by sense used.

Art
Texture craft.

Sensory
Rice bin exploration.

Movement
Yoga poses.

Week 2 – My Five Senses (My Five Senses): Thursday

Circle Time
Talk about hearing.

Literacy
Retell story with props.

Math
Graph favorite senses.

Art
Make sound shakers.

Sensory
Water play for senses.

Movement
Parachute play.

Week 2 – My Five Senses (My Five Senses): Friday

Circle Time
Review our five senses.

Literacy
Draw sense we like best.

Math
Count body parts used for senses.

Art
Make a senses mural.

Sensory
Sensory bottles.

Movement
Dance party.

Week 3 – Friendship & Sharing (Should I Share My Ice Cream?): Monday

Circle Time
Talk about what friends do.

Literacy
Read Should I Share My Ice Cream?.

Math
Count ice cream cones.

Art
Ice cream crafts.

Sensory
Sand tray with scoops.

Movement
Sharing game.

Week 3 – Friendship & Sharing (Should I Share My Ice Cream?): Tuesday

Circle Time
Share about friends.

Literacy
Story sequencing activity.

Math
Number match with cones.

Art
Make friendship bracelets.

Sensory
Water play with scoops.

Movement
Stretching together.

Week 3 – Friendship & Sharing (Should I Share My Ice Cream?): Wednesday

Circle Time
Weather chart & talk about friends.

Literacy
Letter Hunt: I for Ice Cream.

Math
Sort cones by color.

Art
Friendship collage.

Sensory
Playdough cones.

Movement
Yoga partner poses.

Week 3 – Friendship & Sharing (Should I Share My Ice Cream?): Thursday

Circle Time
Talk about sharing.

Literacy
Retell story with puppets.

Math
Graph favorite ice cream.

Art
Cone crafts.

Sensory
Rice bin with cones.

Movement
Parachute play.

Week 3 – Friendship & Sharing (Should I Share My Ice Cream?): Friday

Circle Time
Review sharing week.

Literacy
Draw favorite ice cream.

Math
Count scoops on chart.

Art
Friendship mural.

Sensory
Ice cream sensory bottles.

Movement
Dance party.

Week 4 – Apples & Fall Weather (Apple Trouble): Monday

Circle Time
Talk about apples and fall.

Literacy
Read Apple Trouble.

Math
Count apples.

Art
Apple crafts.

Sensory
Sand tray apple play.

Movement
Apple walk.

Week 4 – Apples & Fall Weather (Apple Trouble): Tuesday

Circle Time
Share about apple picking.

Literacy
Story sequencing activity.

Math
Number match with apples.

Art
Apple prints with paint.

Sensory
Playdough apples.

Movement
Stretching exercises.

Week 4 – Apples & Fall Weather (Apple Trouble): Wednesday

Circle Time
Weather chart & fall talk.

Literacy
Letter Hunt: A for Apple.

Math
Sort apples by color.

Art
Apple collage.

Sensory
Rice bin with apples.

Movement
Yoga apple poses.

Week 4 – Apples & Fall Weather (Apple Trouble): Thursday

Circle Time

Talk about fall leaves.

Literacy

Retell story with props.

Math

Graph apple colors.

Art

Make fall leaf crafts.

Sensory

Water play.

Movement

Parachute play.

Week 4 – Apples & Fall Weather (Apple Trouble): Friday

Circle Time
Review apple week.

Literacy
Draw favorite part of story.

Math
Count fall leaves.

Art
Fall mural.

Sensory
Sensory bottles with leaves.

Movement
Dance party.

Week 1 – Back to School Rules

Book of the Week: David Goes to School

What is your favorite school rule?

Name: _____

Week 2 – My Five Senses

Book of the Week: My Five Senses

Which of your five senses do you like to use most?

Name: _____

Week 3 – Friendship & Sharing

Book of the Week: Should I Share My Ice Cream?

What is something you like to share with friends?

Name: _____

Week 4 – Apples & Fall Weather

Book of the Week: Apple Trouble

What is your favorite thing about fall?

Name: _____

The Nurtured Path – September Preschool Newsletter

September is a month full of learning and exploration! We will practice school rules, explore our five senses, celebrate friendship and sharing, and enjoy the beauty of fall apples and leaves. This month will set the foundation for a fun and engaging school year.

This Month's Themes & Books

• Week 1 – Back to School Rules: David Goes to School

• Week 2 – My Five Senses: My Five Senses

• Week 3 – Friendship & Sharing: Should I Share My Ice Cream?

• Week 4 – Apples & Fall Weather: Apple Trouble

Classroom Highlights

• School murals and rules posters • Taste tests and sense activities • Friendship bracelets and ice cream crafts • Apple prints and fall leaf art

Important Reminders

• Please send extra clothes for sensory play days. • Remember to review school rules at home. • Dress your child for fall weather changes.

Looking Ahead to October

In October, we will dive into pumpkins, leaves, and family celebrations. Fun seasonal activities will keep the excitement for learning going strong.

Thank you for being part of The Nurtured Path family. Let's make this fall full of learning and joy!

October Preschool Curriculum

The Nurtured Path

■ Spooky Fun & Fall Learning ■

Week 1 – Pumpkins & Harvest

Book: Pumpkin Circle

Monday	Welcome Circle	Read story	Counting pumpkins	Pumpkin crafts	Sand tray	Pumpkin walk
Tuesday	Morning Meeting	Story sequencing	Number match	Pumpkin prints	Playdough pumpkins	Stretching
Wednesday	Calendar & Weather	Letter P hunt	Sorting pumpkins	Pumpkin collage	Rice bin	Yoga
Thursday	Sharing Time	Story retell	Graph pumpkin colors	Pumpkin mural	Water play	Parachute play

Friday	Circle Time	Story response	Counting seeds	Harvest mural	Sensory bottles	Dance party

Week 2 – Fall Leaves & Colors

Book: Leaf Man

Monday	Welcome Circle	Read story	Counting leaves	Leaf collage	Sand tray	Leaf walk
Tuesday	Morning Meeting	Story sequencing	Number match	Leaf prints	Playdough leaves	Stretching
Wednesday	Calendar & Weather	Letter L hunt	Sorting leaves	Leaf mural	Rice bin	Yoga

Thursday	Sharing Time	Story retell	Graph leaf colors	Fall tree craft	Water play	Parachute play
Friday	Circle Time	Story response	Counting trees	Fall mural	Sensory bottles	Dance party

Week 3 – Friendship & Fun

Book: Room on the Broom

Monday	Welcome Circle	Read story	Counting brooms	Broom crafts	Sand tray	Pretend play
Tuesday	Morning Meeting	Story sequencing	Number match	Witch hat craft	Playdough brooms	Stretching

Wednesday	Calendar & Weather	Letter B hunt	Sorting animals	Broom collage	Rice bin	Yoga
Thursday	Sharing Time	Story retell	Graph favorite characters	Story mural	Water play	Parachute play
Friday	Circle Time	Story response	Counting stars	Halloween mural	Sensory bottles	Dance party

Week 4 – Family Celebrations & Traditions

Book: The Little Old Lady Who Was Not Afraid of Anything

Monday	Welcome Circle	Read story	Counting shoes	Shoe crafts	Sand tray	Marching game

Tuesday	Morning Meeting	Story sequencing	Number match	Scarecrow craft	Playdough hats	Stretching
Wednesday	Calendar & Weather	Letter H hunt	Sorting clothes	Fall collage	Rice bin	Yoga
Thursday	Sharing Time	Story retell	Graph favorite costumes	Pumpkin craft	Water play	Parachute play
Friday	Circle Time	Story response	Counting costumes	Fall festival mural	Sensory bottles	Dance party

Week 1 – Pumpkins & Harvest

Book of the Week: Pumpkin Circle

Circle Time
Welcome Circle, Morning Meeting, Calendar & Weather, Sharing Time, Pumpkin Talk

Literacy
Read story, Story Sequencing, Letter P Hunt, Story Retell, Story Response

Math
Counting pumpkins, Number Match, Sorting pumpkins, Graph pumpkin colors, Counting seeds

Art
Pumpkin Crafts, Pumpkin Prints, Pumpkin Collage, Pumpkin Mural, Harvest Mural

Sensory
Sand Tray, Playdough Pumpkins, Rice Bin, Water Play, Sensory Bottles

Movement
Pumpkin Walk, Stretching, Yoga, Parachute Play, Dance Party

Week 2 – Fall Leaves & Colors

Book of the Week: Leaf Man

Circle Time
Welcome Circle, Morning Meeting, Calendar & Weather, Sharing Time, Leaf Talk

Literacy
Read story, Story Sequencing, Letter L Hunt, Story Retell, Story Response

Math
Counting leaves, Number Match, Sorting leaves, Graph leaf colors, Counting trees

Art
Leaf Collage, Leaf Prints, Leaf Mural, Fall Tree Craft, Fall Mural

Sensory
Sand Tray, Playdough Leaves, Rice Bin, Water Play, Sensory Bottles

Movement
Leaf Walk, Stretching, Yoga, Parachute Play, Dance Party

Week 3 – Friendship & Fun

Book of the Week: Room on the Broom

Circle Time
Welcome Circle, Morning Meeting, Calendar & Weather, Sharing Time, Friendship Talk

Literacy
Read story, Story Sequencing, Letter B Hunt, Story Retell, Story Response

Math
Counting brooms, Number Match, Sorting animals, Graph favorite characters, Counting stars

Art
Broom Crafts, Witch Hat Crafts, Broom Collage, Story Mural, Halloween Mural

Sensory
Sand Tray, Playdough Brooms, Rice Bin, Water Play, Sensory Bottles

Movement
Pretend Play, Stretching, Yoga, Parachute Play, Dance Party

Week 4 – Family Celebrations & Traditions

Book of the Week: The Little Old Lady Who Was Not Afraid of Anything

Circle Time
Welcome Circle, Morning Meeting, Calendar & Weather, Sharing Time, Family Talk

Literacy
Read story, Story Sequencing, Letter H Hunt, Story Retell, Story Response

Math
Counting shoes, Number Match, Sorting clothes, Graph favorite costumes, Counting costumes

Art
Shoe Crafts, Scarecrow Crafts, Fall Collage, Pumpkin Crafts, Fall Festival Mural

Sensory
Sand Tray, Playdough Hats, Rice Bin, Water Play, Sensory Bottles

Movement
Marching Game, Stretching, Yoga, Parachute Play, Dance Party

Week 1 – Pumpkins & Harvest (Pumpkin Circle): Monday

Circle Time
Discuss pumpkins and fall harvest.

Literacy
Read Pumpkin Circle.

Math
Count pumpkins.

Art
Pumpkin crafts.

Sensory
Sand tray with pumpkin seeds.

Movement
Pumpkin walk.

Week 1 – Pumpkins & Harvest (Pumpkin Circle): Tuesday

Circle Time
Talk about pumpkin growth.

Literacy
Story sequencing activity.

Math
Number match with pumpkins.

Art
Pumpkin prints with paint.

Sensory
Playdough pumpkins.

Movement
Stretching exercises.

Week 1 – Pumpkins & Harvest (Pumpkin Circle): Wednesday

Circle Time

Weather chart & pumpkin talk.

Literacy

Letter Hunt: P for Pumpkin.

Math

Sort pumpkins by size.

Art

Pumpkin collage.

Sensory

Rice bin with seeds.

Movement

Yoga pumpkin poses.

Week 1 – Pumpkins & Harvest (Pumpkin Circle): Thursday

Circle Time
Share favorite pumpkin foods.

Literacy
Retell story with props.

Math
Graph pumpkin colors.

Art
Pumpkin mural.

Sensory
Water play.

Movement
Parachute play.

Week 1 – Pumpkins & Harvest (Pumpkin Circle): Friday

Circle Time
Review pumpkin week.

Literacy
Draw favorite pumpkin activity.

Math
Count pumpkin seeds.

Art
Harvest mural.

Sensory
Pumpkin sensory bottles.

Movement
Dance party.

Week 2 – Fall Leaves & Colors (Leaf Man): Monday

Circle Time
Discuss fall leaves.

Literacy
Read Leaf Man.

Math
Count leaves.

Art
Leaf collage.

Sensory
Sand tray with leaves.

Movement
Leaf walk.

Week 2 – Fall Leaves & Colors (Leaf Man): Tuesday

Circle Time
Talk about colors of leaves.

Literacy
Story sequencing activity.

Math
Number match with leaves.

Art
Leaf prints with paint.

Sensory
Playdough leaves.

Movement
Stretching exercises.

Week 2 – Fall Leaves & Colors (Leaf Man): Wednesday

Circle Time
Weather chart & leaf talk.

Literacy
Letter Hunt: L for Leaf.

Math
Sort leaves by color.

Art
Leaf mural.

Sensory
Rice bin with leaves.

Movement
Yoga leaf poses.

Week 2 – Fall Leaves & Colors (Leaf Man): Thursday

Circle Time
Share about fall activities.

Literacy
Retell story with props.

Math
Graph leaf colors.

Art
Fall tree craft.

Sensory
Water play.

Movement
Parachute play.

Week 2 – Fall Leaves & Colors (Leaf Man): Friday

Circle Time
Review leaf week.

Literacy
Draw favorite leaf activity.

Math
Count trees in pictures.

Art
Fall mural.

Sensory
Leaf sensory bottles.

Movement
Dance party.

Week 3 – Friendship & Fun (Room on the Broom): Monday

Circle Time
Discuss friendship in story.

Literacy
Read Room on the Broom.

Math
Count brooms.

Art
Make broom crafts.

Sensory
Sand tray with stars.

Movement
Pretend play flying on brooms.

Week 3 – Friendship & Fun (Room on the Broom): Tuesday

Circle Time
Talk about characters in story.

Literacy
Story sequencing activity.

Math
Number match with brooms.

Art
Witch hat crafts.

Sensory
Playdough brooms.

Movement
Stretching exercises.

Week 3 – Friendship & Fun (Room on the Broom): Wednesday

Circle Time

Weather chart & broom talk.

Literacy

Letter Hunt: B for Broom.

Math

Sort animals from story.

Art

Broom collage.

Sensory

Rice bin with story items.

Movement

Yoga broom poses.

Week 3 – Friendship & Fun (Room on the Broom): Thursday

Circle Time
Share about friends.

Literacy
Retell story with puppets.

Math
Graph favorite characters.

Art
Story mural.

Sensory
Water play.

Movement
Parachute play.

Week 3 – Friendship & Fun (Room on the Broom): Friday

Circle Time
Review broom week.

Literacy
Draw favorite part of story.

Math
Count stars.

Art
Halloween mural.

Sensory
Star sensory bottles.

Movement
Dance party.

Week 4 – Family Celebrations & Traditions (The Little Old Lady Who Was Not Afraid of Anything): Monday

Circle Time

Talk about family traditions.

Literacy

Read The Little Old Lady Who Was Not Afraid of Anything.

Math

Count shoes in story.

Art

Make shoe crafts.

Sensory

Sand tray with shoes.

Movement

Marching game.

Week 4 – Family Celebrations & Traditions (The Little Old Lady Who Was Not Afraid of Anything): Tuesday

Circle Time

Talk about story characters.

Literacy

Story sequencing activity.

Math

Number match with clothes.

Art

Make scarecrow crafts.

Sensory

Playdough hats.

Movement

Stretching exercises.

Week 4 – Family Celebrations & Traditions (The Little Old Lady Who Was Not Afraid of Anything): Wednesday

Circle Time
Weather chart & costume talk.

Literacy
Letter Hunt: H for Hat.

Math
Sort clothes from story.

Art
Fall collage.

Sensory
Rice bin with clothes.

Movement
Yoga poses.

Week 4 – Family Celebrations & Traditions (The Little Old Lady Who Was Not Afraid of Anything): Thursday

Circle Time
Talk about costumes.

Literacy
Retell story with props.

Math
Graph favorite costumes.

Art
Pumpkin crafts.

Sensory
Water play.

Movement
Parachute play.

Week 4 – Family Celebrations & Traditions (The Little Old Lady Who Was Not Afraid of Anything): Friday

Circle Time
Review celebration week.

Literacy
Draw favorite family tradition.

Math
Count costumes.

Art
Fall festival mural.

Sensory
Sensory bottles with leaves.

Movement
Dance party.

Week 1 – Pumpkins & Harvest

Book of the Week: Pumpkin Circle

What do you like most about pumpkins?

Name: _____

Week 2 – Fall Leaves & Colors

Book of the Week: Leaf Man

What is your favorite thing about fall leaves?

Name: _____

Week 3 – Friendship & Fun

Book of the Week: Room on the Broom

Who would you invite to ride on your broom?

Name: _____

Week 4 – Family Celebrations & Traditions

Book of the Week: The Little Old Lady Who Was Not Afraid of Anything What costume would you wear if you were not afraid?

Name: _____

The Nurtured Path – October Preschool Newsletter

October is a magical month full of pumpkins, colorful leaves, friendship, and traditions. We will celebrate harvest, explore fall nature, enjoy fun Halloween stories, and learn about family celebrations.

This Month's Themes & Books

- Week 1 – Pumpkins & Harvest: Pumpkin Circle
- Week 2 – Fall Leaves & Colors: Leaf Man
- Week 3 – Friendship & Fun: Room on the Broom
- Week 4 – Family Celebrations & Traditions: The Little Old Lady Who Was Not Afraid of Anything

Classroom Highlights

- Pumpkin prints and harvest crafts • Leaf collages and nature walks • Broom crafts and pretend play • Scarecrow crafts and costume fun

Important Reminders

- Please send your child in weather-appropriate clothing for fall. • Costumes are welcome for our special celebration day. • Share family traditions with your child's class to enrich learning.

Looking Ahead to November

In November, we will focus on thankfulness, family, harvest, and community helpers. It will be a time of reflection and celebration together.

Thank you for being part of The Nurtured Path family. We look forward to a festive October full of fun and learning!

November Preschool Curriculum

The Nurtured Path

■ Thankful Hearts & Harvest Learning ■

Week 1 – Thankfulness & Family

Book: The Thankful Book

Monday	Welcome Circle	Read story	Counting blessings	Thankful tree	Sand tray	Gratitude walk
Tuesday	Morning Meeting	Story sequencing	Number match	Family collage	Playdough hearts	Stretching
Wednesday	Calendar & Weather	Letter T hunt	Sorting pictures	Handprint craft	Rice bin	Yoga
Thursday	Sharing Time	Story retell	Graph favorite foods	Thankful mural	Water play	Parachute play

Friday	Circle Time	Story response	Counting friends	Family mural	Sensory bottles	Dance party

Week 2 – Harvest & Food

Book: Feast for 10

Monday	Welcome Circle	Read story	Counting food	Fruit collage	Sand tray	Harvest walk
Tuesday	Morning Meeting	Story sequencing	Number match	Cooking craft	Playdough food	Stretching
Wednesday	Calendar & Weather	Letter F hunt	Sorting foods	Harvest mural	Rice bin	Yoga

Thursday	Sharing Time	Story retell	Graph favorite foods	Veggie prints	Water play	Parachute play
Friday	Circle Time	Story response	Counting food items	Harvest collage	Sensory bottles	Dance party

Week 3 – Community Helpers

Book: Whose Hat Is This?

Monday	Welcome Circle	Read story	Counting hats	Hat crafts	Sand tray	Pretend play
Tuesday	Morning Meeting	Story sequencing	Number match	Helper mural	Playdough hats	Stretching

Wednesday	Calendar & Weather	Letter H hunt	Sorting jobs	Community mural	Rice bin	Yoga
Thursday	Sharing Time	Story retell	Graph favorite helpers	Badge craft	Water play	Parachute play
Friday	Circle Time	Story response	Counting helpers	Hat collage	Sensory bottles	Dance party

Week 4 – Friendship & Sharing

Book: Bear Says Thanks

Monday	Welcome Circle	Read story	Counting bears	Bear crafts	Sand tray	Friend walk

Tuesday	Morning Meeting	Story sequencing	Number match	Friendship cards	Playdough bears	Stretching
Wednesday	Calendar & Weather	Letter B hunt	Sorting foods	Sharing mural	Rice bin	Yoga
Thursday	Sharing Time	Story retell	Graph thankful things	Bear mural	Water play	Parachute play
Friday	Circle Time	Story response	Counting friends	Thankful collage	Sensory bottles	Dance party

Week 1 – Thankfulness & Family

Book of the Week: The Thankful Book

Circle Time
Welcome Circle, Morning Meeting, Calendar & Weather, Sharing Time, Thankful Talk

Literacy
Read story, Story Sequencing, Letter T Hunt, Story Retell, Story Response

Math
Counting blessings, Number Match, Sorting pictures, Graph favorite foods, Counting friends

Art
Thankful Tree, Family Collage, Handprint Craft, Thankful Mural, Family Mural

Sensory
Sand Tray, Playdough Hearts, Rice Bin, Water Play, Sensory Bottles

Movement
Gratitude Walk, Stretching, Yoga, Parachute Play, Dance Party

Week 2 – Harvest & Food

Book of the Week: Feast for 10

Circle Time
Welcome Circle, Morning Meeting, Calendar & Weather, Sharing Time, Harvest Talk

Literacy
Read story, Story Sequencing, Letter F Hunt, Story Retell, Story Response

Math
Counting food, Number Match, Sorting foods, Graph favorite foods, Counting food items

Art
Fruit Collage, Cooking Craft, Harvest Mural, Veggie Prints, Harvest Collage

Sensory
Sand Tray, Playdough Food, Rice Bin, Water Play, Sensory Bottles

Movement
Harvest Walk, Stretching, Yoga, Parachute Play, Dance Party

Week 3 – Community Helpers

Book of the Week: Whose Hat Is This?

Circle Time
Welcome Circle, Morning Meeting, Calendar & Weather, Sharing Time, Helper Talk

Literacy
Read story, Story Sequencing, Letter H Hunt, Story Retell, Story Response

Math
Counting hats, Number Match, Sorting jobs, Graph favorite helpers, Counting helpers

Art
Hat Crafts, Helper Mural, Community Mural, Badge Craft, Hat Collage

Sensory
Sand Tray, Playdough Hats, Rice Bin, Water Play, Sensory Bottles

Movement
Pretend Play, Stretching, Yoga, Parachute Play, Dance Party

Week 4 – Friendship & Sharing

Book of the Week: Bear Says Thanks

Circle Time
Welcome Circle, Morning Meeting, Calendar & Weather, Sharing Time, Friendship Talk

Literacy
Read story, Story Sequencing, Letter B Hunt, Story Retell, Story Response

Math
Counting bears, Number Match, Sorting foods, Graph thankful things, Counting friends

Art
Bear Crafts, Friendship Cards, Sharing Mural, Bear Mural, Thankful Collage

Sensory
Sand Tray, Playdough Bears, Rice Bin, Water Play, Sensory Bottles

Movement
Friend Walk, Stretching, Yoga, Parachute Play, Dance Party

Week 1 – Thankfulness & Family (The Thankful Book): Monday

Circle Time
Talk about what it means to be thankful.

Literacy
Read The Thankful Book.

Math
Count family members or friends.

Art
Make a Thankful Tree.

Sensory
Sand tray with heart shapes.

Movement
Gratitude walk around classroom.

Week 1 – Thankfulness & Family (The Thankful Book): Tuesday

Circle Time
Share what we are thankful for.

Literacy
Story sequencing activity.

Math
Number match with thankful items.

Art
Family collage with pictures.

Sensory
Playdough hearts.

Movement
Stretching exercises.

Week 1 – Thankfulness & Family (The Thankful Book): Wednesday

Circle Time
Weather chart & thankfulness talk.

Literacy
Letter Hunt: T for Thankful.

Math
Sort pictures by family/friends.

Art
Handprint craft.

Sensory
Rice bin with family photos.

Movement
Yoga calm poses.

Week 1 – Thankfulness & Family (The Thankful Book): Thursday

Circle Time
Talk about favorite foods.

Literacy
Retell story with props.

Math
Graph favorite foods.

Art
Thankful mural.

Sensory
Water play.

Movement
Parachute play.

Week 1 – Thankfulness & Family (The Thankful Book): Friday

Circle Time
Review thankfulness week.

Literacy
Draw what you are thankful for.

Math
Count classroom friends.

Art
Family mural.

Sensory
Sensory bottles with glitter.

Movement
Dance party.

Week 2 – Harvest & Food (Feast for 10): Monday

Circle Time
Talk about harvest foods.

Literacy
Read Feast for 10.

Math
Count food items in story.

Art
Fruit collage.

Sensory
Sand tray with food items.

Movement
Harvest walk.

Week 2 – Harvest & Food (Feast for 10): Tuesday

Circle Time
Share favorite foods.

Literacy
Story sequencing activity.

Math
Number match with foods.

Art
Cooking craft.

Sensory
Playdough food.

Movement
Stretching exercises.

Week 2 – Harvest & Food (Feast for 10): Wednesday

Circle Time
Weather chart & food talk.

Literacy
Letter Hunt: F for Food.

Math
Sort foods by type.

Art
Harvest mural.

Sensory
Rice bin with food cards.

Movement
Yoga poses.

Week 2 – Harvest & Food (Feast for 10): Thursday

Circle Time
Talk about family meals.

Literacy
Retell story with props.

Math
Graph favorite foods.

Art
Veggie prints.

Sensory
Water play.

Movement
Parachute play.

Week 2 – Harvest & Food (Feast for 10): Friday

Circle Time
Review harvest week.

Literacy
Draw favorite food.

Math
Count food items.

Art
Harvest collage.

Sensory
Food sensory bottles.

Movement
Dance party.

Week 3 – Community Helpers (Whose Hat Is This?): Monday

Circle Time

Talk about community helpers.

Literacy

Read Whose Hat Is This?.

Math

Count hats.

Art

Hat crafts.

Sensory

Sand tray with hat shapes.

Movement

Pretend play as helpers.

Week 3 – Community Helpers (Whose Hat Is This?): Tuesday

Circle Time
Share about helpers we know.

Literacy
Story sequencing activity.

Math
Number match with hats.

Art
Helper mural.

Sensory
Playdough hats.

Movement
Stretching exercises.

Week 3 – Community Helpers (Whose Hat Is This?): Wednesday

Circle Time
Weather chart & helper talk.

Literacy
Letter Hunt: H for Hat.

Math
Sort jobs from story.

Art
Community mural.

Sensory
Rice bin with tools.

Movement
Yoga helper poses.

Week 3 – Community Helpers (Whose Hat Is This?): Thursday

Circle Time
Talk about favorite helpers.

Literacy
Retell story with props.

Math
Graph favorite helpers.

Art
Badge craft.

Sensory
Water play.

Movement
Parachute play.

Week 3 – Community Helpers (Whose Hat Is This?): Friday

Circle Time
Review helper week.

Literacy
Draw favorite helper.

Math
Count helpers in pictures.

Art
Hat collage.

Sensory
Sensory bottles.

Movement
Dance party.

Week 4 – Friendship & Sharing (Bear Says Thanks): Monday

Circle Time
Talk about friendship.

Literacy
Read Bear Says Thanks.

Math
Count bears in story.

Art
Bear crafts.

Sensory
Sand tray with bear shapes.

Movement
Friend walk.

Week 4 – Friendship & Sharing (Bear Says Thanks): Tuesday

Circle Time
Share things we are thankful for.

Literacy
Story sequencing activity.

Math
Number match with foods.

Art
Friendship cards.

Sensory
Playdough bears.

Movement
Stretching exercises.

Week 4 – Friendship & Sharing (Bear Says Thanks): Wednesday

Circle Time
Weather chart & sharing talk.

Literacy
Letter Hunt: B for Bear.

Math
Sort foods from story.

Art
Sharing mural.

Sensory
Rice bin with bears.

Movement
Yoga friendship poses.

Week 4 – Friendship & Sharing (Bear Says Thanks): Thursday

Circle Time
Talk about being thankful for friends.

Literacy
Retell story with props.

Math
Graph thankful things.

Art
Bear mural.

Sensory
Water play.

Movement
Parachute play.

Week 4 – Friendship & Sharing (Bear Says Thanks): Friday

Circle Time
Review friendship week.

Literacy
Draw something you share.

Math
Count friends in class.

Art
Thankful collage.

Sensory
Sensory bottles with hearts.

Movement
Dance party.

Week 1 – Thankfulness & Family

Book of the Week: The Thankful Book

What are you thankful for?

Name: _____

Week 2 – Harvest & Food

Book of the Week: Feast for 10

What food do you like to eat with your family?

Name: _____

Week 3 – Community Helpers

Book of the Week: Whose Hat Is This?

What community helper do you want to be?

Name: _____

Week 4 – Friendship & Sharing

Book of the Week: Bear Says Thanks

What do you like to share with your friends?

Name: _____

The Nurtured Path – November Preschool Newsletter

November is a time to reflect on thankfulness, celebrate family, and enjoy the harvest season. We will explore community helpers, practice gratitude, and learn the value of friendship and sharing.

This Month's Themes & Books

• Week 1 – Thankfulness & Family: The Thankful Book

• Week 2 – Harvest & Food: Feast for 10

• Week 3 – Community Helpers: Whose Hat Is This?

• Week 4 – Friendship & Sharing: Bear Says Thanks

Classroom Highlights

• Thankful tree and family collages • Harvest crafts and veggie prints • Helper hats and community murals • Friendship cards and bear crafts

Important Reminders

• Please note holiday schedule changes for November. • Share family traditions or favorite foods with the class. • Dress children in warm clothing as the weather cools.

Looking Ahead to December

In December, we will celebrate winter, holidays, and family traditions with festive activities and stories. It will be a joyful way to end the year together.

Thank you for being part of The Nurtured Path family. Let's make this November full of gratitude and joy!

December Preschool Curriculum

The Nurtured Path

❄■ Winter Wonders & Holiday Joy ■

Week 1 – Winter Weather

Book: The Snowy Day

Monday	Welcome Circle	Read story	Count snowflakes	Snow painting	Snow sensory bin	Snow walk
Tuesday	Morning Meeting	Story sequencing	Number match	Snow collage	Playdough snow	Stretching
Wednesday	Calendar & Weather	Letter S hunt	Sorting snow items	Snow mural	Rice bin	Yoga
Thursday	Sharing Time	Story retell	Graph snowy days	Snow globe craft	Water play	Parachute play

Friday	Circle Time	Story response	Count mittens	Winter mural	Sensory bottles	Dance party

Week 2 – Holidays Around the World

Book: Celebrations Around the World

Monday	Welcome Circle	Read story	Count countries	Flag crafts	Sand tray	Holiday walk
Tuesday	Morning Meeting	Story sequencing	Number match	Cultural collage	Playdough symbols	Stretching
Wednesday	Calendar & Weather	Letter C hunt	Sorting holidays	Holiday mural	Rice bin	Yoga

Thursday	Sharing Time	Story retell	Graph favorite holidays	Festival craft	Water play	Parachute play
Friday	Circle Time	Story response	Count candles	Celebration mural	Sensory bottles	Dance party

Week 3 – Kindness & Giving

Book: The Mitten

Monday	Welcome Circle	Read story	Count animals	Mitten craft	Sand tray	Mitten walk
Tuesday	Morning Meeting	Story sequencing	Number match	Animal collage	Playdough animals	Stretching

Wednesday	Calendar & Weather	Letter M hunt	Sorting animals	Mitten mural	Rice bin	Yoga
Thursday	Sharing Time	Story retell	Graph favorite animals	Mitten sharing craft	Water play	Parachute play
Friday	Circle Time	Story response	Count mittens	Winter mural	Sensory bottles	Dance party

Week 4 – Winter Animals

Book: Over and Under the Snow

Monday	Welcome Circle	Read story	Count animals	Animal crafts	Sand tray	Animal walk

Tuesday	Morning Meeting	Story sequencing	Number match	Animal collage	Playdough animals	Stretching
Wednesday	Calendar & Weather	Letter A hunt	Sorting animals	Animal mural	Rice bin	Yoga
Thursday	Sharing Time	Story retell	Graph favorite animals	Snow animal craft	Water play	Parachute play
Friday	Circle Time	Story response	Count tracks	Winter mural	Sensory bottles	Dance party

Week 1 – Winter Weather

Book of the Week: The Snowy Day

Circle Time
Welcome Circle, Morning Meeting, Calendar & Weather, Sharing Time, Snow Talk

Literacy
Read story, Story Sequencing, Letter S Hunt, Story Retell, Story Response

Math
Counting snowflakes, Number Match, Sorting snow items, Graph snowy days, Counting mittens

Art
Snow Painting, Snow Collage, Snow Mural, Snow Globe Craft, Winter Mural

Sensory
Snow Sensory Bin, Playdough Snow, Rice Bin, Water Play, Sensory Bottles

Movement
Snow Walk, Stretching, Yoga, Parachute Play, Dance Party

Week 2 – Holidays Around the World

Book of the Week: Celebrations Around the World

Circle Time
Welcome Circle, Morning Meeting, Calendar & Weather, Sharing Time, Holiday Talk

Literacy
Read story, Story Sequencing, Letter C Hunt, Story Retell, Story Response

Math
Counting countries, Number Match, Sorting holidays, Graph favorite holidays, Counting candles

Art
Flag Crafts, Cultural Collage, Holiday Mural, Festival Craft, Celebration Mural

Sensory
Sand Tray, Playdough Symbols, Rice Bin, Water Play, Sensory Bottles

Movement
Holiday Walk, Stretching, Yoga, Parachute Play, Dance Party

Week 3 – Kindness & Giving

Book of the Week: The Mitten

Circle Time
Welcome Circle, Morning Meeting, Calendar & Weather, Sharing Time, Kindness Talk

Literacy
Read story, Story Sequencing, Letter M Hunt, Story Retell, Story Response

Math
Counting animals, Number Match, Sorting animals, Graph favorite animals, Counting mittens

Art
Mitten Craft, Animal Collage, Mitten Mural, Mitten Sharing Craft, Winter Mural

Sensory
Sand Tray, Playdough Animals, Rice Bin, Water Play, Sensory Bottles

Movement
Mitten Walk, Stretching, Yoga, Parachute Play, Dance Party

Week 4 – Winter Animals

Book of the Week: Over and Under the Snow

Circle Time
Welcome Circle, Morning Meeting, Calendar & Weather, Sharing Time, Animal Talk

Literacy
Read story, Story Sequencing, Letter A Hunt, Story Retell, Story Response

Math
Counting animals, Number Match, Sorting animals, Graph favorite animals, Counting tracks

Art
Animal Crafts, Animal Collage, Animal Mural, Snow Animal Craft, Winter Mural

Sensory
Sand Tray, Playdough Animals, Rice Bin, Water Play, Sensory Bottles

Movement
Animal Walk, Stretching, Yoga, Parachute Play, Dance Party

Week 1 – Winter Weather (The Snowy Day): Monday

Circle Time
Talk about snow and winter weather.

Literacy
Read The Snowy Day.

Math
Count snowflakes.

Art
Snow painting craft.

Sensory
Snow sensory bin with cotton balls.

Movement
Pretend snow walk.

Week 1 – Winter Weather (The Snowy Day): Tuesday

Circle Time
Discuss how snow feels.

Literacy
Story sequencing activity.

Math
Number match with snow items.

Art
Snow collage.

Sensory
Playdough snow.

Movement
Stretching exercises.

Week 1 – Winter Weather (The Snowy Day): Wednesday

Circle Time
Weather chart & snow talk.

Literacy
Letter Hunt: S for Snow.

Math
Sort snow items by size.

Art
Snow mural.

Sensory
Rice bin with snowflakes.

Movement
Yoga snow poses.

Week 1 – Winter Weather (The Snowy Day): Thursday

Circle Time
Talk about snowy days.

Literacy
Retell story with props.

Math
Graph snowy days.

Art
Snow globe craft.

Sensory
Water play with ice cubes.

Movement
Parachute play.

Week 1 – Winter Weather (The Snowy Day): Friday

Circle Time
Review snow week.

Literacy
Draw favorite snowy day activity.

Math
Count mittens.

Art
Winter mural.

Sensory
Snow sensory bottles.

Movement
Dance party.

Week 2 – Holidays Around the World (Celebrations Around the World): Monday

Circle Time
Talk about different holidays.

Literacy
Read Celebrations Around the World.

Math
Count countries visited in book.

Art
Flag crafts.

Sensory
Sand tray with holiday symbols.

Movement
Holiday walk around class.

Week 2 – Holidays Around the World (Celebrations Around the World): Tuesday

Circle Time
Share family traditions.

Literacy
Story sequencing activity.

Math
Number match with holiday items.

Art
Cultural collage.

Sensory
Playdough holiday symbols.

Movement
Stretching exercises.

Week 2 – Holidays Around the World (Celebrations Around the World): Wednesday

Circle Time
Weather chart & holiday talk.

Literacy
Letter Hunt: C for Celebration.

Math
Sort holidays by type.

Art
Holiday mural.

Sensory
Rice bin with flags.

Movement
Yoga holiday poses.

Week 2 – Holidays Around the World (Celebrations Around the World): Thursday

Circle Time
Talk about favorite holidays.

Literacy
Retell story with props.

Math
Graph favorite holidays.

Art
Festival craft.

Sensory
Water play.

Movement
Parachute play.

Week 2 – Holidays Around the World (Celebrations Around the World): Friday

Circle Time
Review holiday week.

Literacy
Draw favorite holiday tradition.

Math
Count candles or lights.

Art
Celebration mural.

Sensory
Sensory bottles with glitter.

Movement
Dance party.

Week 3 – Kindness & Giving (The Mitten): Monday

Circle Time
Talk about kindness and giving.

Literacy
Read The Mitten.

Math
Count animals in story.

Art
Mitten craft.

Sensory
Sand tray with mitten shapes.

Movement
Mitten walk.

Week 3 – Kindness & Giving (The Mitten): Tuesday

Circle Time
Share about giving to others.

Literacy
Story sequencing activity.

Math
Number match with animals.

Art
Animal collage.

Sensory
Playdough animals.

Movement
Stretching exercises.

Week 3 – Kindness & Giving (The Mitten): Wednesday

Circle Time
Weather chart & mitten talk.

Literacy
Letter Hunt: M for Mitten.

Math
Sort animals by size.

Art
Mitten mural.

Sensory
Rice bin with animal figures.

Movement
Yoga mitten poses.

Week 3 – Kindness & Giving (The Mitten): Thursday

Circle Time
Talk about sharing.

Literacy
Retell story with props.

Math
Graph favorite animals.

Art
Mitten sharing craft.

Sensory
Water play.

Movement
Parachute play.

Week 3 – Kindness & Giving (The Mitten): Friday

Circle Time
Review mitten week.

Literacy
Draw favorite part of story.

Math
Count mittens.

Art
Winter mural.

Sensory
Sensory bottles.

Movement
Dance party.

Week 4 – Winter Animals (Over and Under the Snow): Monday

Circle Time
Talk about animals in winter.

Literacy
Read Over and Under the Snow.

Math
Count animals in story.

Art
Animal crafts.

Sensory
Sand tray with animal tracks.

Movement
Animal walk.

Week 4 – Winter Animals (Over and Under the Snow): Tuesday

Circle Time
Share favorite winter animals.

Literacy
Story sequencing activity.

Math
Number match with animals.

Art
Animal collage.

Sensory
Playdough animals.

Movement
Stretching exercises.

Week 4 – Winter Animals (Over and Under the Snow): Wednesday

Circle Time
Weather chart & animal talk.

Literacy
Letter Hunt: A for Animal.

Math
Sort animals by type.

Art
Animal mural.

Sensory
Rice bin with animal figures.

Movement
Yoga animal poses.

Week 4 – Winter Animals (Over and Under the Snow): Thursday

Circle Time
Talk about how animals survive winter.

Literacy
Retell story with props.

Math
Graph favorite animals.

Art
Snow animal craft.

Sensory
Water play.

Movement
Parachute play.

Week 4 – Winter Animals (Over and Under the Snow): Friday

Circle Time
Review winter animals week.

Literacy
Draw favorite winter animal.

Math
Count tracks in snow.

Art
Winter mural.

Sensory
Sensory bottles with snow.

Movement
Dance party.

Week 1 – Winter Weather

Book of the Week: The Snowy Day

What do you like to do in the snow?

Name: _____

Week 2 – Holidays Around the World

Book of the Week: Celebrations Around the World

What holiday do you celebrate with your family?

Name: _____

Week 3 – Kindness & Giving

Book of the Week: The Mitten

What animal would you put inside the mitten?

Name: _____

Week 4 – Winter Animals

Book of the Week: Over and Under the Snow

What winter animal is your favorite?

Name: _____

The Nurtured Path – December Preschool Newsletter

December is a joyful month filled with winter wonders, holidays around the world, kindness, and animals in the snow. We will explore traditions, create festive crafts, and practice kindness and sharing.

This Month's Themes & Books

- Week 1 – Winter Weather: The Snowy Day
- Week 2 – Holidays Around the World: Celebrations Around the World
- Week 3 – Kindness & Giving: The Mitten
- Week 4 – Winter Animals: Over and Under the Snow

Classroom Highlights

• Snow painting and winter murals • Holiday flag crafts and cultural collages • Mitten crafts and sharing activities • Winter animal crafts and pretend play

Important Reminders

• Please dress children in warm clothing for outdoor play. • Note holiday schedule changes this month. • Share family traditions or winter activities with the class.

Looking Ahead to January

In January, we will start the new year with themes of snow fun, resolutions, and winter learning. It will be an exciting start to a fresh year of exploration.

Thank you for being part of The Nurtured Path family. Let's make December full of joy and wonder!

www.ingramcontent.com/pod-product-compliance
Lightning Source LLC
Chambersburg PA
CBHW051325110526
44582CB00004B/106